To R.G.
With love from
Louise

St. James of Jerusalem
2005

ACCIDENTS OF FORTUNE

Andrew Devonshire

ACCIDENTS OF FORTUNE

MICHAEL RUSSELL

First published in Great Britain 2004
by Michael Russell (Publishing) Ltd
Wilby Hall, Wilby, Norwich NR16 2JP

Reprinted (twice) 2004

Typeset in Sabon by Waveney Typesetters
Wymondham, Norfolk
Printed and bound in Great Britain
by Biddles Ltd, King's Lynn, Norfolk

ISBN 0 85955 286 1

FOR DEBO

Contents

༽

Acknowledgements

❧

My wife, Debo, as always with anything concerning Chatsworth, has been invaluable. My secretary, Helen Marchant, for whom no praise is too high, has been of incalculable assistance – liaising with Michael Russell over an extended period of editorial suggestion and counter-suggestion, checking endless details of fact, organising the supply of illustrations, and conjuring up relevant information that might otherwise have slipped the net. Gill Coleridge and John Saumarez Smith have given constant support; and Nicholas Smith, of Currey & Co, has cast his professional eye over my account of our protracted negotiations over my father's estate, in which his firm played such a crucial role. I have referred to the Oliver family and others in the text, but I should like to say how outstandingly fortunate I have been in the services of all the staff at Chatsworth and our other family estates, in particular the services of a series of Agents – Hugo Read, Derrick Penrose, and now Roger Wardle and his able deputy Nick Wood. And finally I must record my gratitude to Ian Else, surveyor, Andrew Peppit, archivist, and Ian Fraser Martin, photographer, for their particular help.

Publisher's Note

꒰ঌ

Park Top: A Romance of the Turf by Andrew Devonshire (see pp. 96–7) was first published by London Magazine Editions in 1976 and reissued in paperback by John Murray in 2000.

Family Tree

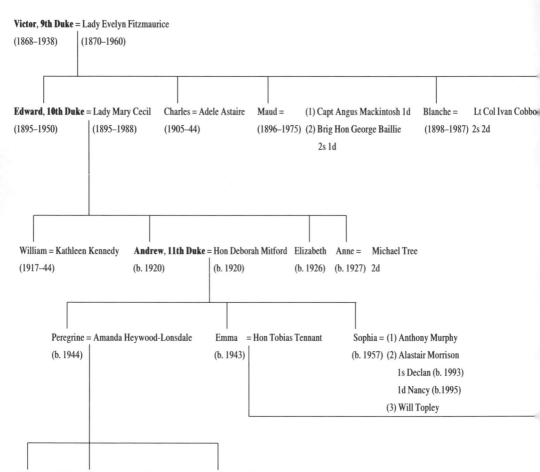

Victor, **9th Duke** = Lady Evelyn Fitzmaurice
(1868–1938)   (1870–1960)

Edward, 10th Duke = Lady Mary Cecil   Charles = Adele Astaire   Maud =   (1) Capt Angus Mackintosh 1d   Blanche =   Lt Col Ivan Cobbo
(1895–1950)   (1895–1988)   (1905–44)   (1896–1975) (2) Brig Hon George Baillie   (1898–1987) 2s 2d
                                                      2s 1d

William = Kathleen Kennedy   **Andrew, 11th Duke** = Hon Deborah Mitford   Elizabeth   Anne =   Michael Tree
(1917–44)   (b. 1920)   (b. 1920)   (b. 1926) (b. 1927) 2d

Peregrine = Amanda Heywood-Lonsdale   Emma   = Hon Tobias Tennant   Sophia = (1) Anthony Murphy
(b. 1944)   (b. 1943)   (b. 1957) (2) Alastair Morrison
                                                  1s Declan (b. 1993)
                                                  1d Nancy (b.1995)
                                                  (3) Will Topley

William (b. 1969) Celina (b. 1971) = Alexander Carter Jasmine (b. 1973) = Nicholas Dunne

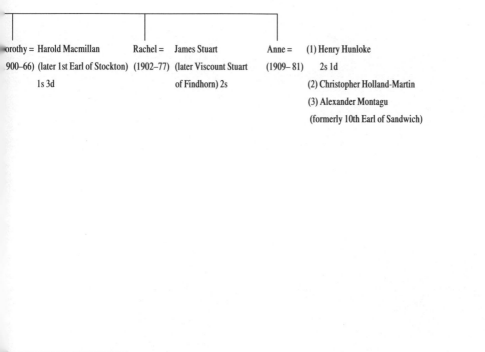

orothy = Harold Macmillan   Rachel = James Stuart   Anne =   (1) Henry Hunloke
900–66) (later 1st Earl of Stockton) (1902–77) (later Viscount Stuart   (1909–81)   2s 1d
       1s 3d   of Findhorn) 2s   (2) Christopher Holland-Martin
                                                                        (3) Alexander Montagu
                                                                        (formerly 10th Earl of Sandwich)

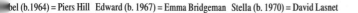

bel (b.1964) = Piers Hill   Edward (b. 1967) = Emma Bridgeman   Stella (b. 1970) = David Lasnet

Starting Out

❧

I was born in London on 2 January 1920 at my maternal grand-father's house, 20 Arlington Street. He later moved next door to no. 21, and no. 20 is now part of the Ritz Hotel. His father, Lord Salisbury, had been Prime Minister and in a society where the upper classes had still the upper hand, my parental combination of Cavendish and Cecil was a strong start. Social position was still largely an accident of birth. I'd concede that there were some fairly serious accidents, but because people who are able to open doors are usually rather good at closing them, the system was successfully self-perpetuating. Certainly there were more free spirits in that post-First War era, but the smart clubs and the smart regiments clung to the generational *déjà-vu*. Nowadays, of course, our world is radically changed. The aristocracy of celebrity – in theory at least – is attainable by people from all beginnings. Whereas poor old dukes are considered more freakish by the day.

My father was not yet a Member of Parliament, and he and my mother spent much of their time at Hardwick Hall, and the rest in their London house at 2 Upper Belgrave Street. Sadly, I have no memories of those early years at Hardwick. But because Hardwick at that period was surrounded by coalmines, it suffered from – today's phrase – a degree of soot pollution. So, when I was four, my parents decided to move to a comparatively modest house called Churchdale, a mile up the hill from the village of Ashford in the Water and five miles north west of Chatsworth. There was a drawing room, dining room, my father's sitting room, one spare sitting room called the Green Room, the school room, three visitors' bedrooms, and, by modern standards, a shortage of bathrooms.

The house was approached through a woody shrubbery where my father planted literally thousands of snowdrops and winter aconites. He was a gardener with green fingers, while my mother had the conventional taste for herbaceous borders. The garden was about four acres with lawns and a particularly fine beech tree and was a joy from spring to autumn. There was a kitchen garden in which my father grew specie daffodils, about which he became very knowledgeable. He also succeeded in growing hibiscus, an achievement in the Peak District. Alongside the stables there was an orchard where he grew colchicums.

It was a happy house. Our upbringing was not an exercise in social science. My parents were good and reasonable people who merely accommodated the presence of children with their way of life. We had a French governess who gave us morning lessons in the school room from nine to twelve. In the afternoons we were left to our own devices, not influenced by our parents. There were two horses at Churchdale, looked after by a groom called Sidney, and I rode a good deal (hunting came later). There was also a tortoise which went slowly about its business of being our pet. We had our own garden plots, where I grew annuals, and a hut in the woods where my brother Billy and I would play for hours – it had that double advantage of the outside den: children like its secrecy, parents like knowing where the children are.

My two sisters were not yet born. I was two years younger than Billy; Elizabeth did not appear until six years after me, and Anne a year after that. As I got older I became conscious of the full implications of primogeniture. But my father was a firm believer in the principle, on the grounds that however harsh it might seem, it was the only way of maintaining a great estate. He was right.

In generations past it had been possible to hive off parts of a family's wealth to provide for younger sons. From the end of the First World War virtually no estate could afford to be so denuded. I am a believer in the great estates and in the landlord and tenant system. I also believe that everything should be done to keep a great art collection together. Having said that, primogeniture is a hard system for younger sons. They are brought up with all the privileges of their elder brother, only to find that when they have to stand on their own feet, the amount of family wealth bestowed on them is, in terms of natural justice, far too little. For this reason I do not altogether regret having only one son, and he likewise.

There cannot be a compromise; my father's overriding ambition was to keep the family's estates intact. It was ironic that he died four months before the works of art and family fortune would legally have passed to me and I was faced with punitive death duties on all that contributed to the family's wealth, including land, works of art and investments.

My father was elected MP for West Derbyshire in the snap election called by Baldwin at the end of 1923 and remained MP for the constituency until he succeeded my grandfather in 1938. He planted the election voting results in crocuses – blue for Tory, yellow for Liberal, purple for Labour. He was a delightful, slightly eccentric man with idiosyncratic views on many subjects. He once said to me, 'Andy, you will find whenever there is trouble in the world, there is always a clergyman behind it'; and at the end of his life he warned me that homosexuality, which had been a complete taboo in his father's time (and most of his), was becoming increasingly fashionable and might well, in my time, become compulsory. He was appallingly dressed (his tailors bore the suitable name of Cutter & Rook), made do quite happily with paper collars, and his wardrobe included a very surprising pair of shoes that were half leather and half suede – the like of which I have never seen elsewhere.

Over the family fortune he was completely unassuming. My brother and I were not aware of the extent of the family's possessions. The drawing room at 2 Carlton Gardens, which became our London house, had three paintings by Rembrandt and two by Franz Hals – they had previously been in Devonshire House – but no reference was ever made to them. Certainly my father showed no inclination to add to the art collection: the only items I can recollect him buying were a pair of narwhal horns and a model ship made by French prisoners of war in about 1800. His dominant interests were the House of Commons, salmon fishing in Ireland, shooting and gardening. Because of his enthusiasm for shooting I was taught to shoot at the customary age of twelve by the head keeper at Chatsworth, Mr Maclauchlan, a revered figure. I was a hopeless shot, while my brother was a good one. As soon as my father died I abandoned it for ever.

Both my parents positively disliked horse racing, although my father's younger brother, Charlie Cavendish, had horses in Ireland and therefore retained the all-straw colours that are the oldest registered on the Turf. On one occasion, in the 1920s, my mother and father were asked to stay at Windsor Castle for Royal Ascot. In those days there was a royal procession back from the course as well as to it. My mother forgot the return journey. This reached Queen Mary's ears and, probably to my parents' relief, they were not asked to Windsor for Royal Ascot again.

My father was a tremendous admirer of the Jewish community. I remember Chaim Weizmann used to come to our house in London. His had been one of the articulate, persuasive voices of Zionism which had done much to bring about the Balfour Declaration in 1917, and he was to become the President of the State of Israel in 1948. My father's enthusiasm was out of line with the then prevalent anti-Semitism of the majority of his class. He went further: it was a genuine source of regret to him that there was no detectable Jewish blood in the Cavendishes and he envied my mother's family, the Cecils, for having some, albeit rather distant. I inherited this admiration for the Jewish community and when I was a member of the Conservative Party I was President of the Conservative Friends of Israel group. I have paid eight visits to Israel, was lucky enough to befriend the long-time mayor of Jerusalem, the remarkable Teddy Kollek, and, a little surprisingly, I even had a forest in Galilee named after me. I must admit I haven't followed my arboreal fortunes. I hope I haven't been felled and made into picnic tables.

My father also had his antipathies. One of these was the Liberal Prime Minister of Canada, Mackenzie King. At the time of the fall of France in 1940 my father was Under-Secretary of State for Dominion Affairs. A civil servant asked him if he might be considering sending his two young daughters to Canada for the duration of the war – he would presumably still have connections there as his father had been Governor-General. 'Send my daughters to Canada?' said my father. 'I'd rather they were brought up under Hitler than Mackenzie King.'

My grandfather had indeed been Governor-General of Canada, from 1916 to 1921, and was thereafter Secretary of State for the Colonies for two years. He was at Chatsworth when we moved to Churchdale, but in 1925 he suffered a severe stroke, which had the effect of sadly changing his character. Until then, I understand, he had been an easy-going, ironic, laconic man; after his stroke he was very bad-tempered and difficult to get along with. Billy and I were not popular. Years later my mother explained to me that she felt it was because we looked more like her family than the Cavendishes that my grandfather so disliked us and always alluded to us as 'the brats'. As a result, in the days of my childhood we found Chatsworth an unhappy place.

My grandmother cannot have had an easy time. She is hard to assess; she was very good with small children, but as soon as they got to be ten or twelve she was far too critical. If it was so of her grandchildren, I believe it was equally true of her children. After his stroke my grandfather and she hardly spoke to each other. There was a saint-like figure called Elsie Saunders, who acted as the go-between. She had been my grandmother's secretary when they were in Canada. She returned to England with them and lived at Chatsworth until my grandfather died in 1938.

My brother and I, with our father and mother, attended very painful lunches at Chatsworth with my grandparents and Elsie. It didn't help that, except at large parties, my grandparents used a room called the Small Dining Room. It is without doubt the gloomiest room at Chatsworth. It faces north, the ceiling is too high and it is grim.

Proceedings were not improved either by my grandmother's eccentric taste in food. She had an excellent cook, and the food on grand occasions was superb. At these lunches, however, she used to experiment with new dishes, dishes she thought economical. We were once confronted with lambs' tails.

To make matters worse, since his stroke my grandfather, having been initially very fond of my mother, had taken against her. This made her understandably agitated during these ordeals with the result that my father, already ill at ease, also got very irritated with her. My brother and I remained silent and frightened.

Once a year, however, Chatsworth became really alive. This was at Christmas, though I do not think my mother enjoyed it – she never felt comfortable with my grandmother. My grandparents had two sons and five daughters, and year by year all, with the exception of my father's younger brother, Charlie, came to Chatsworth. Year by year the number of grandchildren grew. At its zenith there were twenty-one and the house hummed with activity. Over a hundred people slept under its roof, many of them in what would now be considered unacceptable conditions.

Since then I have talked to retired people on the estate who worked in the house during that time and they all say that, although the work at Christmas was very hard, it was a happy time. Other than at Christmas, my grandmother used to have the occasional large weekend party, with up to forty guests – quite a number of whom arrived and left without meeting each other. These gatherings were held in the summer, and I only witnessed them as a small boy before I went to school. My main recollection of them is of flowers in the drawing rooms and library. How much the guests enjoyed themselves I don't know, but anyone interested in pictures, books, silver and gold plate would have had a field day.

After five years with the long-suffering governess, I followed my brother away to school at Ludgrove. I enjoyed my four years there, although the school gave prominence to games and I was not much good at either cricket or football. In fact I was rotten at football and my sporting high point was to squeak into the cricket 2nd XI and scratch twenty-five edgy runs on the leg side against the neighbouring school, Elstree (where, by coincidence, I was to be stationed in the Army in 1941). But the teaching was good, and the school worked closely with Eton, so we were well prepared for the entrance exam; with the result that I passed into Eton at a level above my ability.

The headmaster of Ludgrove was called Mr Oakley, unmarried and unceremoniously given the nickname of 'Po'. The second master, who had a very pretty wife, was Mr Henley. He was a decent tenor and used to sing in the school concerts which marked the end of every term. He particularly favoured 'The Soldiers of the Queen'. I can hear him now.

There was a predictable figure in charge of the gymnasium who answered to 'Sergeant Major', and strutted about in a muscular, disciplined way. It was he who introduced me to boxing, which I continued at Eton and Sandhurst. Again I wasn't much good, but I had the advantage both of being a lightweight and having very long arms to fend off my opponents.

The school library was rather like the food – quite appetising boys' stuff, from Henty to Percy F. Westerman, with titles like *Chums of the Golden Vanity*, full of principled endeavour, and, a little incongruously, a good collection of books on the Roman Empire.

I arrived at Eton in January 1933. My housemaster was Mr Powell and his house overlooked the main football ground known as 'The Field'. He was a keen mountaineer and in the middle of the summer holidays in my first year he was killed, with three other housemasters and a member of the science staff, in an accident in the Bernina Alps. Hubert Hartley took over my house. His amusing wife, Grizel, was a considerable asset.

From the school's point of view I was less so. I was lucky to last the course. I was dirty, lazy, and always on the borderline of failing in trials (the Eton word for examinations). I did, however, achieve rather questionable status in becoming in 1936 the school book-maker – only to hit the buffers at Royal Ascot the following year when Ticca Gari won the King's Stand Stakes at 5–1.

Notwithstanding this rather salutary mishap, my enthusiasm for racing was undiminished. I managed to get to Kempton Park races on two or three occasions, but I was seen there by a fortunately generous-minded master, who merely warned me not to go again or he would have to tell my housemaster. But my most enterprising venture was to get to Newmarket on a school holiday to see the July Cup. Little could I have imagined that just over sixty years later one of my horses, Compton Place, would win it.

My reports for the summer term – or 'half' as we called it – of 1937 were exceptionally bad and included the fact that I owed £100 (a lot of money in those days) in the town. I was very apprehensive about my father's reaction – the dire view of my work and the mention of the financial trouble might make him very angry indeed. But luck was with me. At the end of the summer half the OTC went to camp on Salisbury Plain. The weather was hot, resulting in shirt-sleeve order. I lay on a noxious weed and my bare arms swelled up. On reporting sick, I was sent home. I arrived at our London house to find it deserted but on the hall table a letter to my father in Hubert Hartley's writing, clearly containing the dreaded documents. I didn't have the courage to tear it up, but I hid it under a bust on the hall table. It was never seen again.

As it happened, the last thing my father would have been thinking about while grouse shooting on his Yorkshire moors would have been my school reports. So nothing was said. There was a bad moment when my mother, driving me to catch the train back to school, said she hadn't seen the previous half's reports, but I brushed it off with 'Oh, I'm afraid they weren't good.' When I got back, Hubert Hartley asked me about my father's reaction to the reports and the money I owed. I told him my father was very busy as a Minister of the Crown and no doubt had other things on his mind.

My good luck continued. I backed two horses to win the Autumn Double, the Cambridgeshire and the Cesarewitch. They were named Artist's Prince and Punch. They both won and my financial problem was solved. I left that December without distinction. The personification of, in the Eton vernacular, a 'scug'.

Into War

❧

My parents were divided over the dominant events of 1938 – the German occupation of the Sudetenland and the Munich crisis. My father was a member of Chamberlain's Government and supported the Prime Minister. Privately, my mother sided with her brother, then Lord Cranborne (later Lord Salisbury), one of the leaders of the opposition to Chamberlain. Happily, my brother and I were spared serious family political rows over the issue as my mother was prepared to subjugate her feelings and – on the surface at least – appear loyal to my father.

I took my father's view and got involved in passionate arguments. Over the days of the Munich crisis I was staying with Sir Hugh Shaw-Stewart at Ardgowan in Renfrewshire. I was sharing a room with someone not politically minded and the wretched man had to listen to hour after hour of my arguments and opinions. At four in the morning Sir Hugh himself intervened in a Jaeger dressing gown to remonstrate that bleak though the situation was, everyone deserved some sleep.

As to the rights and wrongs, it is hard to assess whether the Germans or Britain and her allies gained more from the delay in the outbreak of war. Of one thing I am certain – Chamberlain would have received far less approbation had he not used those fatal words 'Peace for our time … Peace with honour.' Years after those tragic events the gossip was that when handed the bit of paper on which the words were written, he said he didn't like them, they weren't his style. But whoever thought of the words, Chamberlain used them.

I was about to start my first term at Cambridge. Towards the end of the summer holidays I was sent to a family in Lyons to learn French, at which I singularly failed. The fact was that I and my circle of friends were resigned to the inevitability of war and used it as an excuse for our frivolous approach to life. And Cambridge, in those prewar days, was a very congenial platform for our almost professional indolence. Newmarket, conveniently nearby, was an added joy: I was a regular racegoer and I have never lost my affection for it.

After my Eton career you might wonder how I had actually got into Cambridge. It was the result of some undisclosed and underhand collusion between Eton and the college selected for me, Trinity. I lived in digs on the outskirts of the town, attended no lectures and did no work. Soon after my arrival I had the good fortune to be elected a member of the Athenaeum Club and spent much of my time there. The club premises, with dining room and a pleasant, good-sized sitting room, were opposite Trinity Main Gate. We played cards and drank too much – a horse's neck (brandy and ginger ale) was a favoured drink. Even the club tie of pink and white stripes (which I still sometimes wear) was something of a statement.

At the end of my first year a slight cloud appeared in this untroubled sky. Examinations. There was precious little to examine, but even the indulgent authorities of those days had to impose some requirements. To avert general embarrassment, Fate, ever resourceful, involved me in a serious motor accident. We were returning late one night from London and the car overturned on top of me, permanently damaging a kidney (fortunately my other one has soldiered on quite adequately). My two companions escaped without injury. I was confined to Addenbrooke's Hospital for a month, by which time the exams had safely been and gone. I emerged to join in that frenetic 'last Season' in London in the shadow of impending war.

The fashionable nightclub was the 400 in Leicester Square. Both Billy and I were regulars; and it was patronised too by my father. Owing to the complications of the then licensing laws you could not order individual drinks direct but had to have bottles of alcohol in your name. My father, who was a Government Minister under his courtesy title Lord Hartington, thought it slightly indecorous to have a line of bottles blaring out the name Hartington, so he decided to have them designated with the names of fish beginning with 'h'. Billy and I cottoned on to this and used to trawl for herring, haddock, halibut or hake with a compliant barman.

We returned to Chatsworth in time for my brother's twenty-first birthday celebrations in August 1939, postponed for some months because the house was not ready. The atmosphere had something of the Duchess of Richmond's ball before the Battle of Waterloo. It was a sumptuous occasion, with the estate tenants and employees joining in the reception with a host of our friends who were staying in the house. We sensed it was the closing of an age. In a final reprieve Billy and I went to stay at Castle Howard for the York race meeting. Our friend Mark Howard was the eldest son and it was a memorable party. We knew now that war must come in weeks if not days, and there was a determination to enjoy every moment to the full.

I am not proud of my lack of enterprise following the outbreak of war. I did what I was told, waiting to be called up, but a man of spirit would surely have managed to enlist – as the more adventurous of my friends had already done. As it was, I returned to Cambridge, now a very different place. There were no visits to London, no Athenaeum and no Newmarket. I moved into much better digs close to Trinity. I had to attend regular Corps activities. Luckily I had two very good friends in the same situation, Richard Stanley (Lord Derby's younger brother) and John Wyndham (later Lord Egremont); but I was ashamed of not being in the Army. My feelings were not helped by Pansy, Lady Digby saying to me when I met her that December 'What, Andrew? Still not in uniform?'

Unfortunate it may have been, but it had compensations. It set my life in a better perspective. In my first year the real Cambridge had hardly impinged on me. Now, with petrol rationing and other restrictions, I lived the proper life of an undergraduate. I got to know a wider range of people and became involved in undergraduate societies. Cambridge, from being a location for the sybaritic life, became a university. And I was glad to be part of it.

My call up came in June. I was to join the Guards Depot at Caterham. I had ten days between Cambridge and going to the depot. I went first to Derbyshire – Debo was there too and we became unofficially engaged.

We had met one May evening the previous year – at dinner before going on to a dance. In fact I remembered seeing her three or four years before at Eton when she had chosen to dye her hair very bright yellow. I thought her very beautiful as I watched her walking round the cricket pitch. So our meeting in that restaurant before the dance was love at second sight. At least for me; I can't vouch for Debo. The restaurant was off Piccadilly, not far from my present London house, and it still gives me a frisson when I pass to see people eating and drinking there.

After those few days in Derbyshire I went to my parents' house in Carlton Gardens. By a quirk of construction it was possible to communicate via the wastepipes between the bathrooms, and that morning my father and I happened to be having our baths at the same time. By this unusual means of communication he called out 'You've chosen a good day to join the Army. France is out of it. We now have a good chance of winning.' It wasn't everyone's reading of the situation, but just at that moment he had reason to trust fortune. Billy had been in France and hadn't arrived back with the Dunkirk contingents. There were several very anxious days and then good news. He had got out of France from St Nazaire. I was with my parents when we had the relief of knowing he was safe.

I reported to Caterham. The discipline was renowned for its severity. At the end of my first day I was on my way back to the block where I slept, innocently eating an apple I had bought in the NAAFI, when a drill sergeant shouted at me and struck me on the shoulder with his pace stick for daring to take the liberty of eating on the parade ground.

I cannot pretend I enjoyed my weeks as a guardsman, but they undoubtedly did me a great deal of good. I arrived as a thoroughly spoilt young man. Now I was treated like any other recruit to the Brigade and spoilt we were not. There was a lot of drill and a lot of physical training. We longed for the less severe parts of the curriculum, like talks on regimental history – though these took place after lunch when one was at risk of falling asleep.

There were twenty-eight of us in the barrack room. Also sleeping in the barrack room was a regular guardsman known, and addressed, as 'trained soldier'. It was his job to teach us how to polish our boots to the required standard, how to polish the brass links of our webbing equipment and our cap stars until they were bright enough to shave in. I learnt the tricks of the trade. The chief one was to cover one's wet boots with boot polish and then set fire to them. This removed the polish, in a dramatic way, but dried the boots. And this made it easier to reapply the polish. Only the Army could devise such a quaintly logical regenerative process.

The barrack room had to be immaculate. Everyone was responsible for his own 'bed area', the area immediately surrounding his bunk. The trick was to push all the dust around your bunk into your neighbour's space. And then make sure he pursued the same practice to the neighbour one further away. You were liable, too, to be allocated other specific responsibilities: cleaning the stove was bad, dusting the light bulbs 'cushy'.

Once a week there was a kit inspection, when everything had to be laid out to a precise formula, cleaned, creased and folded. The inspection was carried out by an officer. To ensure that the creases were immaculate, I used to pile the relevant items under the three square 'biscuits' which formed the mattress of one's bunk. The result was an enormous mound under your bedding which made for an uncomfortable night; it was rather like lying upside down on a small camel. The following morning you laid out your kit with its determined creases and hoped it would not attract criticism. If it did, dispiritingly – after all the conscientious effort – you were 'idle'. The military were not great ones for shades of criticism.

Those weeks at Caterham taught me something I was to discover to be profoundly true in the years ahead: it is not so much what one has to do that matters but with whom one does it. Although treated as any other guardsmen, we were known as the 'Brigade Squad' and provided we did not disgrace ourselves we were to go on to Sandhurst and then be commissioned. Being in a kindred group like that made the physically arduous training much more easily sustainable. I made several permanent friends among my twenty-seven companions there, not least Philip Toynbee, who had the particular virtue of being even more incompetent than I was.

The daylight air raids were beginning and we saw German aircraft overhead. Normally on leaving Caterham and going on to Sandhurst there was a week's leave. Now, owing to the seriousness of the situation, we were given just twelve hours. We went to London and spent those hours as we thought best.

I took a female companion to lunch at the Mirabelle and then to the cinema. When we all reassembled at Waterloo in the early evening, we found that Philip, who had clearly spent his time in the pub, was extremely drunk. We saw that he came to no mischief in the train and got him safely onto the truck that met us. On the short drive to Sandhurst we continued to keep an eye on him and all was well until we turned into the gates. Our attention must have been distracted by what was to be our new home because to our dismay, by the time we had drawn up at the Royal College's New Building, where we were to be quartered, Philip had taken off all his clothes. The reaction of the senior warrant officer who met us showed the Brigade at its best. The drill sergeant in charge took one look at Philip and sent for a stretcher and blanket. Having found out his name he had him carried to his room. There was no further reference to the episode; indeed Philip became something of a star when the instructors found out that he had fought in the Spanish Civil War. They asked him to give a lecture, because he had first-hand experience of combat which the great majority of them had not. Considering how unmilitary Philip was and they the epitome of the Brigade, we thought it reflected considerable credit on them.

Philip had hoped to go into the Welsh Guards, but the powers that be recognised he was more suited to the Intelligence Corps. This resulted in him attending the School of Intelligence based at what had been Smedley's Hydro in Matlock, now the offices of Derbyshire County Council. I arranged for Philip to go and dine with my father at Churchdale, which proved a resounding success as they both had an affection for port.

After Caterham, Sandhurst was much more relaxed. Discipline was less severe, and though the PT and drill sessions were not my idea of fun, much of the other work was interesting. We were taught military strategy and tactics, which involved exercises riding bicycles through the Surrey countryside and finishing up at a pub. We were also able to get up to London quite often, provided we were back at a given hour. I also made other expeditions to local hostelries and the homes of friends when the day's training was over.

My group of cadets finished training at Sandhurst in November. The days preceding the end of the course were an anxious time as I waited on what kind of report I would be given. There were four categories: A – excellent, B – passable, C – not good and D – disastrous. I managed a B. This was considered adequate for me to join the regiment I had chosen, the Coldstream Guards, in which Billy was already serving. We were given ten days' leave before we joined up. Debo and I chose that moment to become officially engaged.

The first months as a junior officer were remarkable, particularly coming after the rigours of Caterham and the discipline of Sandhurst. I was appointed to a holding battalion stationed at Regent's Park Barracks, London. The barracks had been condemned in 1904, but still remained doggedly in use although there was virtually nothing to do. Two drills in the morning and, unless you were picket officer, that was it for the day. London could still keep up its spirits, in spite of the Blitz being at its height, and I was often out into the small hours. It was a strange time. The Blitz *per se* was an appalling experience, with horrific loss of life, to say nothing of the huge destruction of property. For all that, it was a time of unification for those who lived in London, as it was for those who lived in the other cities that suffered heavy bombardment. The Germans made a psychological error in those bombings, because apart from the damage they did, which was not serious enough to knock us out of the war, the Blitz brought the feeling that everyone was in it together. Millions were in the front line. It improved morale. People, as so often in this country in times of adversity, put aside their existing barriers of easier times and worked together for the common cause.

The creation of The Home Guard had just the same effect. Class distinction was swept aside. The retired were given a sense of responsibility and purpose. The social nuances of 'Dad's Army', quite apart from their entertainment value, are perfect.

Debo and I got married on 19 April 1941. The Blitz, though moderating from its worst, continued with very heavy raids on London. Social life, however, was not easily floored. The wedding was on a Saturday and a remarkable number of friends and family were able to come to the service at St Bartholomew the Great in the City and the reception at my father-in-law's house in Rutland Gate, the windows of which had been blown out during a raid the previous night. Debo's mother hung strips of wallpaper at the windows to make curtains. We spent our honeymoon at Compton Place, my family's house in Eastbourne. It was curious being there. The German bombers en route for London flew over the town. Every night of our week there we heard the planes droning overhead and returning some hours later.

Shortly after our honeymoon I was posted to a newly formed battalion, the 5th, which in due course became part of the Guards Armoured Division. It was a frustrating time of military inactivity and boredom and it lasted two and a half years.

There was one highlight while I was still in London. A detachment from our regiment at Regent's Park Barracks was sent to guard Winston Churchill when he was at Chequers. He was a friend of my parents and, on learning I was there, asked me to dine. The chosen date, 27 May 1941, coincided with the sinking of the *Bismarck* after a chase in the Atlantic involving a large number of

British warships. *Bismarck* had sunk the battleship HMS *Hood* a few days before and the Navy's success was a much-needed fillip to morale at home. It was a thrilling evening. Messages kept coming in from naval headquarters giving updates on the chase, so the Prime Minister was either pressing me to second helpings or divulging the news reports. By the time I took my leave the *Bismarck* had been sunk.

Years later I saw him at dinners at The Other Club, of which he was a founder member (I think in response to not being elected to its more distinguished counterpart, The Club), and in his latter years our paths occasionally crossed on the racecourse. He told me that his political career had just overlapped with that of the 8th Duke of Devonshire, politically better known as Lord Hartington. He said that on one occasion they were driving to address a mass meeting of some 5,000 people in Liverpool. Hartington asked Churchill 'Are you nervous?', to which he replied 'Yes' – this was the first time he had spoken to such a large audience. Hartington said, 'Don't be nervous. I used to be, but when I rose to speak at a similar event at the Corn Exchange in Manchester, I thought to myself I had never seen so many damned fools in front of me and I have never been nervous since.' His attitude is reflected in a cartoon entitled 'The Treasury Bench', which hangs in my bathroom, of Joseph Chamberlain, Gladstone and Hartington: 'Lord Hartington ... is a decent gentleman who yawns at his own speeches, prizes the triumphs of the turf and the boudoir above those of the forum, and rather has been commissioned into political life as the Agent and Sentry of the Aristocracy, than has entered upon it because he feels any especial capacity for dealing with public affairs ...'

The new 5th Battalion was initially stationed in Hertfordshire. Later we went to camp in Siegfried Sassoon's park at Heytesbury, just outside Warminster in Wiltshire. He could often be seen walking in the park dressed in a blue blazer and grey flannel trousers. He kept himself to himself but I can't believe he was thrilled that his boundary wall which ran along the main road was constantly being knocked into rubble by some inaccurately driven armoured vehicle.

Debo and I lived in a small house in Warminster. The owner regarded it as his war work to provide married quarters at a token rent for a serving soldier. A delightful maid called Gladys was included in this generous gesture. We were domestically fortunate in those summer months of 1941 and we were very happy, although the military side of my life was hardly fulfilling. We had the additional good fortune of having Daphne Weymouth living nearby. Married to the future Lord Bath, who was in the Middle East, she had a house near Longleat called Sturford Mead where her entertaining showed few signs of wartime privation. One of her regular guests was Evelyn Waugh, which led to an unexpected friendship between us.

With Debo now expecting a child, we decided to set up a first home of our own. It was a small house called The Rookery in Ashford in the Water, close to Churchdale, and we stayed there until 1947.

Possibly the lowest point in those years of military boredom and inactivity was November 1942. As the battalion's mortar officer I was sent to Singleton in West Sussex for a month's training with live ammunition. The platoon was stationed at Singleton railway station, the station where King Edward VII arrived when staying with the Duke of Richmond for Goodwood Races. I lived at Drovers Hotel in the village and I was startled when the Archbishop of Canterbury, William Temple, came for a short stay, which suggested the authorities must be getting nervous. I hated using live ammunition, as I was fearful of errant missiles killing livestock or even humans who had strayed onto the range, which was not clearly enough defined. To make matters worse the weather was foul. My commanding officer, who had a low opinion of my ability, paid repeated visits to see how we were getting on. I was greatly relieved, and a little surprised, that we survived the four weeks there without casualties.

At the weekends I would go up the hill and walk the racecourse.

In the paddock I found the big case of boards containing the names of the jockeys of the day – heroes of mine like Gordon Richards, Brownie Carslake, Harry Wragg and Dick Perryman. After the war I became a regular racegoer at Goodwood and always looked wistfully across at that area where I suffered those painful experiences as mortar officer. It gave an extra dimension to the pleasures of the racing. Goodwood has always been a very special favourite of mine. It is a sadness that I have not yet managed to win a race there. But I still have hopes.

So the peripatetic round of training and preparation continued into 1943. But preparing for what? We tried to analyse the war news to see where we might be needed, aware that our fate could be a permanent training role at home. The regiment had distinguished itself in the fighting in North Africa. For me, however, the good moments were domestic and social. Debo was able to join me at Hunstanton in Norfolk, and later, when we had a spell in the York-shire Wolds, Richard and Virginia Sykes entertained us royally at Sledmere. Then, finally, the word came through that I was to be posted to the 3rd Battalion; and that meant service overseas.

Active Service

꩜

The 3rd Battalion Coldstream Guards, to which I was now to be transferred, had been in Egypt at the outbreak of war and had taken a prominent and distinguished part in the battles of the Western Desert, while suffering severely at Tobruk. With the North African campaign successfully concluded in Tunisia, they were sent next to Italy, where their landing at Salerno in September 1943 coincided with the news of the Italian surrender. If they hoped this would smooth their path they underestimated the determination of the German resistance. Nevertheless the Fifth Army occupied a sadly battered Naples at the beginning of October and the Germans fell back on their main Winter Line. This included the stronghold of Cassino, to be the scene of perhaps the bitterest close-quarter fighting of the whole Italian campaign. But barring even the approach to the Winter Line, in those closing weeks of 1943, was Monte Camino; and on the southern side of Monte Camino was a two-mile slope graphically nicknamed 'Barearse', where the battalion endured a gruelling and tactically unproductive four days. The continuous rain made it impossible to maintain supply lines, the objective had not been accomplished and morale was temporarily dented.

My companions and I had reported in November for embarkation from the Forth of Clyde in a convoy that took some days to assemble. So we were initially on board in a state of limbo. One memory in particular remains with me. Early one evening the *Queen Mary* slipped past us down the river. She was in use as a troopship and, although we knew that the U-boat threat in the Atlantic had been very significantly reduced, there was something uplifting and defiant about the sight of her powering silently away into the dusk.

The voyage to Naples took three weeks. We first headed west out into the Atlantic before turning south-east for the Mediterranean. As we approached the Straits of Gibraltar, the captain told us over the loudspeaker that we were now sailing through the waters where Trafalgar had been fought. He made it sound like a morale-booster and you couldn't dispute it had been a good result, but we suspected it might not give us immunity against the Germans.

So it turned out. Once we came through the Straits we were warned that German reconnaissance aircraft had spotted the convoy and it was likely we would be attacked from the air the following evening. Apparently the favourite hour for such an attack was as the sun was setting behind the Atlas Mountains. Sure enough, the German planes appeared on cue, causing great excitement among the senior naval officers, who took a professional interest in the weaponry. I think the Germans had some aerial torpedoes, though as mere soldiery I'm afraid our only concern was that the new hardware, whatever it was, shouldn't land on us. The scene was spectacular, with the aircraft weaving against the sun going down, and the noise deafening – non-stop gunfire from the convoy's naval escort and bombs exploding. Our ship was lucky. The vessel next to us was hit and sunk. It was difficult to establish facts but the casualties were heavy, including many nurses going out to serve in Italy.

We stopped briefly at one port in North Africa. We were not allowed to leave the ship, but a small party was sent ashore to buy citrus fruit. This had been an almost forgotten luxury in wartime England. When the shoppers came back and distributed their haul, I ate sixty-three tangerines, which may be a record and should have given me enough vitamins to last me the war.

We arrived and disembarked in Naples harbour. We had the good fortune to see the famous bay under ideal conditions of early morning sunshine. Once disembarked, we were taken to a transit camp in the garden of a former royal palace just outside the city. We spent some wet and frustrating days there, the only redeeming features a profusion of cyclamen neapolitanum and a heart-stopping camellia in full blossom against a palace wall. My father's enthusiasm for gardening struck a chord.

Eventually we were sent in lorries to our respective units. I, and one or two friends, joined the 3rd Battalion. It was not an easy moment to join. Between their landing at Salerno and the end of the year, the battalion had lost 144 killed and 350 wounded, in addition to the inroads of malaria. There were only a handful of the desert veterans left and, as the official history puts it, 'men who had joined at Tripoli now ranked as old soldiers'. The bonds of such shared experience are very strong: nice as we found our new companions, we felt something of outsiders.

We were facing the main enemy defences in the Garigliano valley. On 23 January 1944 an Allied force landed at Anzio, just south of Rome, and established a bridgehead. We, meanwhile, were having an uncomfortable time around Trimonsuoli, with foul weather and being constantly shelled and mortared. Then four days' welcome rest out of the line before another miserable week at Trimonsuoli, with a steady erosion of casualties and bleak physical conditions. At Tufo, in February, conditions were better and in March we were relieved by the Americans and went south to rest in Sorrento.

Also in Sorrento were men of the 24th Guards Brigade, resting after heavy fighting at Anzio. These included Bill De L'Isle and Dudley, a Grenadier, who had just received the VC as a result of his part in it. Again I have a cameo picture of our meeting. A hot day, a meadow with a profusion of wild flowers, he the hero, I very much the admiring junior. Our meeting was the beginning of a lifelong friendship.

Much-needed reinforcements arrived to bring the battalion up to strength. With so many new arrivals, I no longer felt a new boy, though hardly a veteran after only three months in action. When we returned to the line in April, our situation, too, was incomparably improved from the winter miseries. The Germans were seven miles away, contact was by long-range patrol, artillery exchanges were the exception rather than the rule. I remember we were sitting in sunshine on a hillside one morning at the end of April when a beaming Tom Egerton appeared from Battalion HQ to tell me that Debo had had a son.

In May the savage assault on Monte Cassino began and the stronghold finally capitulated on the 18th. We were not involved. The horrors of such grinding, close-quarter fighting had something in common with Stalingrad. The German flank collapsed and both the Fifth and the Eighth Armies began the advance on Rome. The city fell on 4 June. Two days later came news of the Normandy landings.

I was fortunate in that my company entered Rome in the morning – a battalion column had driven through in the hours of darkness – and I shall never forget the intoxication of it all. There were crowds on the streets, we were showered with flowers, and, best of all, the city was intact. It was my first visit there, and never could it have looked so radiant.

So now we had to push on north. On 8 June Commanding Officer's orders announced: '3 Coldstream Guards will capture Florence.' It was an instruction, though not, as it turned out, an accurate forecast.

While I may have been unlucky in my commanding officer in England, in Italy it was just the opposite. George Burns, 'Colonel George' as he was known to all, was everything a CO should be: never asking a subordinate to undertake a task he would not do himself, as considerate to the most newly joined guardsman as to his second in command, and always cheerful. I am bound to him by a special link, in that but for his tolerance I should have been court martialled and disgraced.

During the course of the advance between Rome and Florence each company took turn and turn about to lead, thus being in closest touch with the enemy. The golden rule in such situations is that 'stand to' is ordered. This means that all troops stand to their arms from an hour before dawn until an hour after. On one occasion when the company under my command was in the lead, I was convinced the Germans had retreated and 'stand to' could be disregarded. I informed the company sergeant major, somewhat to his surprise, and then retired to a convenient bush hoping for a good night's sleep.

I was roused by the sound of Colonel George shouting at me. Had I ordered 'stand to'? Half asleep, I admitted I hadn't. I like to think my answer would have been the same had I been fully alert. And just as well, as he had already obtained the facts from the sergeant major. He gave me the ticking off I deserved, but said that at least I had told the truth and so he would take the matter no further.

From Rome we pushed on northwards against an ever-weakening opposition. The occasional skirmish with the enemy, the occasional bombardment, but it could only be described as an ambling advance. We had been attached as the infantry brigade of the 6th South African Armoured Division. They proved both gallant and delightful companions. They also produced large quantities of South African brandy. Taken in moderation it was a good tonic, but too much left one feeling extremely ill.

Progress was steady. As infantry we were involved in a lot of footslogging along dusty roads and across country, some of it up steep hillsides, even mountains. It also got very hot. However, there were compensations: the lovely countryside, terraced vineyards, and a profusion of fruit – cherries, apples, pears, grapes and, best of all, figs. I even remember one or two days marching through mulberry groves where the trees were being grown for silkworms.

Three cameos stand out during this part of the advance. The first was when I was walking along the side of the road with my sergeant major and we came across a dismembered foot and ankle. Being squeamish, I looked away. Not so my sergeant major. He gave it a hearty kick and it squelched aside to reveal a pair of German binoculars which he immediately snatched up. His more robust attitude had earned them, but I couldn't resist some covetous glances.

The second episode was late one afternoon. We had had a long slog uphill in the heat. We came to what we thought was a deserted farmhouse, which usually meant the enemy was not far away. Enticingly, there was a well. Having posted scouts to watch in case there were any Germans in the vicinity, we got some buckets and the company had a marvellous time sluicing each other down.

Suddenly we heard footsteps and the soldiers were seizing their rifles when around the corner came a beautiful young Italian girl, heavily pregnant. No doubt her family, frightened at the prospect of being caught in the conflict, had felt that she would be an encumbrance to their escape. Be that as it may, here was this poor deserted girl, alone and within hours of giving birth. Our medical officer arranged for her to be taken back to safety and delivered of her child.

The third episode was when we were in a battle between Rome and Florence. Both tanks and infantry were involved, and the noise of gunfire was everywhere. Some thirty yards away I saw a German soldier eating sandwiches under a tree. I drew my service revolver and fired at him, several times. I'm no Wyatt Earp, but some of the bullets must have gone fairly close. He showed not the slightest reaction. He must have been eating either the best or the worst sandwiches in the history of sandwich-making. They had his total attention. In disgust I hurled the revolver towards him. Before leaving the Army I had to pay £30 for losing that revolver. But I'm glad now I missed him when I fired.

Fifteen miles south of Florence, near a village called Strada, I had some anxious moments. My company's objective, a hill half a mile in front of the village, cost us a third of our strength. Worse, when we finally made it, we found that the Germans were still on the summit above us and we had to dig in under heavy mortar fire. No 1 Company managed to get up behind us and evacuate the casualties, but couldn't deliver rations or water. So there we had to stay for a night and a hot July day, making do with our emergency rations and whatever remained in our water bottles, while the Germans worked round through the woods on our left and began to snipe at us from the rear. In the evening the Scots Guards managed to clear the left flank and we scuttled back into reserve.

At the beginning of August we were on the very last lap before Florence.

The Germans blew the bridges over the Arno, and it was the Scots Guards not ourselves who took the southern part of the city and then, over several days of street fighting, finally prised the Germans out on the other side of the Arno. We drove back to Siena for three weeks' rest. Our casualties since the advance on Rome had been 53 killed and 156 wounded. The brigade had advanced 270 miles in 64 days. An unrecorded statistic is that during that time I did not have a single bath and was infested with fleas.

A word on the business of fighting. The efficacy of different regiments certainly varied. The so-called 'good' regiments drew their strength principally from the quality of their non-commissioned officers, and that must imply there was a regimental expectation of which both tradition and training were ingredients. As for the officers themselves, they were even more susceptible to this same expectation: chosen originally as much for some social connection as for their latent powers of leadership, I suspect much of the apparent bravery was fear of cowardice. It's difficult, for instance, to see how Guards subalterns on the Western Front in the First World War could otherwise have coped with the statistical chances of going over the top. It was a sort of social programming, heroic and tragic. Which is why witnessing fear in others was so disturbing, because fear is contagious.

What I can vouch for personally was the camaraderie. We were totally bound up, during our active service, with the fortunes of each other, ready to reproach ourselves for the loss of our friends. Luck is unpredictable. I remember once our position was being very heavily shelled. I asked my sergeant, Sergeant King, to stay where he was while I looked over the rim of a hill about a hundred yards away to see if there was any sign of the enemy. I'm sure he thought I was being commendably officerly – the danger would seem to lie in exposing oneself in moving forward. Yet when I returned the dear good man had been killed by a shell that had landed in our dugout just after I left it. That sort of memory nags away at you. Happily, through my letter of condolence to his wife, I became a friend of his son, now a distinguished Cambridge academic.

One of the best books in my view ever written about the First World War, *In the Cannon's Mouth* by P. J. Campbell, describes how on his first leave from the Western Front, although glad of the comfort of England after the trenches and the happiness of seeing his family, his thoughts were still of his battery. I went on leave after the fall of Florence. Together with several others I went down to the Sorrento Peninsula, to Positano. It should have been a paradise, but we found that our thoughts were continually with our comrades hundreds of kilometres to the north.

While on leave in the south we saw a vast assemblage of ships, both warships and mercantile. At the time we did not know their purpose, but later learnt that they were to transport the forces that invaded the south of France. On returning to my unit and the continuing advance north, it was immediately noticeable that our forces had been depleted. The punch had been taken out of our attack. It was easy to speculate afterwards that had we been able to advance faster with our original strength, the capture of Trieste might have been achieved; and that might have affected the whole disposition of the Iron Curtain countries. It is a theory reassuringly rejected by one of our erstwhile Coldstream platoon commanders, the distinguished professor of war studies Sir Michael Howard.

As we resumed operations, the partisans began to play a more prominent role. When we were involved with the capture of Montecatini Alto, a hilltop village above the popular spa of Monte-catini, hordes of men carrying small triangular red flags appeared as if out of the ground. The Germans were nowhere to be seen except for a dejected gaggle of deserters.

It was at Montecatini, in early September 1944, that I was told that my brother had been killed by a sniper's bullet in Belgium. The news brought more than shock and grief. I preferred not to dwell on the implications of becoming my father's heir. Besides, Billy and Kick had been married in May and for all I knew Kick might be pregnant. It was a sensitive and extremely distressing situation. Fortunately perhaps, my total involvement with the battalion and the campaign in hand restricted my horizons. What I might or might not be doing when peace came and I returned to life in England was not an immediate consideration.

Our advance continued at a slow pace. Just before we reached Bologna I was sent for by the adjutant and told that I was to return to a training camp south of Naples. I was very put out. Had I done something wrong? I was assured not, but the reason was not divulged.

Some months later I discovered what lay behind it. Uncle Harold Macmillan, who was then Resident Minister with Cabinet status at General Alexander's HQ, saw fit to ask the GOC – an old friend – that I should be withdrawn from my battalion. It was kindly meant and must have given relief to my mother and father. But personally, when I discovered the truth, I bitterly resented it.

I spent three miserable months in a ghastly camp. It never stopped raining. I felt bored and ashamed. I had just been promoted to the rank of major but military progress seemed irrelevant. In the spring of 1945 the battalion as a whole was sent back to England. Before it left I rejoined it, and I remember all too clearly meeting my friends and feeling unable to look them in the eye.

However, returning to England brought great joys. I was reunited with my family, and saw my son for the first time. I was posted to Pirbright for the last months of the war, but my political ambitions were indulged with time off. More important, I could begin to make my mind up about my peacetime persona.

Inheritance

※

In the autumn of 1950 my father sent me to Australia. He was keen on investing in the Dominions and my remit was to explore the possibilities. At the end of November I received two telegrams – the first saying my father was dangerously ill, followed almost immediately by a second saying that he had died. He was fifty-five. In fact he had died instantaneously but my mother thought that sending two telegrams would soften the shock. His untimely death completely reshaped my life. His overwhelming ambition had been that the Cavendish estates and fortune should be kept intact. Accordingly, my elder brother having been killed in action, he had taken the necessary steps for all that he owned to devolve on to me. The legal machinery was set in motion as soon as the war was over.

There had been new Government legislation which stipulated that shares in a private company controlled by an individual would no longer qualify for the 45% estate duty relief on agricultural land. Accordingly, in March 1946 my father transferred the £2,225,000 of shares he owned in Chatsworth Estates Co to a new discretionary trust, the Chatsworth Settlement, one of whose joint trustees was his wife. I quote from John Pearson's *Stags and Serpents* (1983): 'But because the Duke was relatively young, and there were financial advantages in keeping the shares temporarily in the Estates Company, the transfer was kept in escrow. It was stipulated that it was to be signed by the trustees if the Duke's life was thought to be "in special danger" – making it legally binding at his death.' (After 1946 my father was fond of saying that the only antiques he owned were the extremely ancient clothes he stood up in.)

The law at that time laid down that five years must elapse from the date of handing over property for it to become free of death duties. It followed that my father must live until March 1951 before I could inherit without having to pay duty, the top rate of which was increased in 1948 to a swingeing 80%. My father went to church virtually every Sunday and used to tell me that it was then he ticked off another week. When he died there were still fourteen weeks to tick and the crucial document was still unsigned. I was then faced with the problem of raising millions of pounds.

I must, for the record, give a brief summary of what was involved. The total agreed value of Chatsworth Estates Co assets was £9m and the duty owed £4.72m, with interest payable at £1,000 per day. There was very little public sympathy at the time for tax planning which failed.

When my father died he owned 120,000 acres (just larger than the Isle of Wight), but much of it was moorland used for shooting or agricultural land let to tenant farmers with an average annual rent of less than 1% of the estimated total value of the land. He also owned Chatsworth, Hardwick Hall, Compton Place in Eastbourne, Bolton Abbey in Yorkshire, and their contents, plus mineral rights in Derbyshire and ground rental income from Eastbourne and Buxton. I already owned Lismore Castle, which I had inherited from my father's younger brother Charlie (see 'Ireland').

Three options presented themselves. I could sell up everything immediately, pay what I owed and live a comfortable life free from all these problems of debt; I could follow our Librarian Francis Thompson's idea to preserve Chatsworth by making it an outpost centre of the arts for the University of Manchester; or I could sell selectively and retain some of my father's estate.

As soon as I got back from Australia a meeting of the six agents was called: three from Derbyshire, one from Yorkshire, one from Eastbourne and one from a Scottish estate of 26,000 acres my father had bought during the war. It was to be the first of many meetings held at Curreys' offices in 21 Buckingham Gate in London. Messrs Currey & Co have looked after my family's affairs, both legal and financial, for generations. Framed photographs of former Dukes of Devonshire punctuate the pervasive décor of bound volumes of law reports. It is a room designed to cast down the blithest of spirits at the happiest of times. Even today, when my family affairs are on a reasonably even keel, that room still fills me with depression. In the winter of 1950 it was an ideal setting for meetings that looked likely to result in the end of the Devonshire fortunes. Yet it was Curreys' acumen, and in particular that of the then senior partner, Dugald Macpherson, that saved the day. Perhaps, too, Curreys' furnishings have mystical powers. My friend and Curreys' present senior partner Nicholas Smith (Dugald's nephew), reading this, reminds me that I once said I had taken all the most important decisions in my life when sitting looking at a particular hole in Curreys' carpet and had asked that neither the carpet nor any other feature of the room should be altered during my lifetime.

The first decision taken was that each section of my father's property – land, works of art and stocks and shares – should find its own share of the total burden.

I played no part in the sale of stocks and shares. On what land and works of art were to be disposed of I took the lead. We decided that the Scottish estate, the most recently acquired, should be the first to go. Thousands of acres in Derbyshire followed, but the bulk of the Eastbourne and Yorkshire estates were kept intact. The most fascinating part of the negotiations, however, was over the works of art. I could either sell the bulk and retain the best, or sell the best and keep the bulk. I decided on the latter.

The family's finest treasures found their way to the major national institutions. To the British Museum – the Greek bronze head of Apollo, the *Liber Veritatis* of Claude Lorrain, the ninth-century Benedictional of St Aetholwold, a Van Dyck Italian sketch-book, and around 140 early books (mostly incunabula, 60 of which were printed before 1500, including 14 works by Caxton's head printer, Wynkyn de Worde, of which the British Museum then had no copies); to the National Portrait Gallery – Holbein's cartoon of Henry VII and VIII; to the National Gallery – the Memling Triptych, Rembrandt's *The Philosopher*; to the Walker Art Gallery in Liverpool – Rubens's *The Holy Family*; and to the Victoria and Albert Museum – the fifteenth-century Devonshire hunting tapestries.

It is a matter of satisfaction that nothing left the country. I also accept that the Benedictional was too important to remain in a private collection. However, I deeply regret the loss of the Holbein cartoon. The authenticity of various paintings of Henry VIII by this artist all have some qualifications, whereas there is no doubt as to the genuineness of the cartoon. Claude's sketchbook too is sadly missed, since the veracity of any Claude painting is proven by its inclusion in the sketchbook. The loss of the Memling Triptych, the jewel in the crown of the Devonshire pictures, was a grievous blow. I cannot pretend I miss the tapestries, and, in spite of the disposal of books, the Chatsworth library remains a fine one. The departure of the Rembrandt to the National Gallery turned out fortunately for the estate (if not for the nation), since it has now been demoted to 'school of the artist', while the two that remain at Chatsworth (*Portrait of an Old Man* and *King Uzziah*) have their reputations intact.

This was not the end of the disposals of land and works of art. Further depredations followed in the years to come. Remarkably there was no demand for part or whole of Chatsworth's collections of Old Master drawings. These remained intact, although for a variety of other reasons a number have been disposed of during the last forty years. I have often wondered why the British Museum, the National Gallery or the V & A did not show an interest in acquiring some of the collection.

Progress was slow. In those days interest on duty owed was 2%, while you could invest at a considerably higher rate. It was much to my advantage to pay as slowly as possible. My advisers adopted a simple yet ingenious manoeuvre to delay payments. During the long correspondence with the Inland Revenue they noted just how many days elapsed between the date they wrote and the Revenue replied. They then deferred replying to that letter until one day short of the same interval. This enabled them to spin out the nego-tiations, while making it impossible for the Revenue to accuse them of dragging their feet.

We were over half way through 1954 and the settlement problems were still unresolved. On 12 August that year I was on the train to London. It had stopped at Bedford station. It was not quite St Paul on the road to Damascus or Archimedes' *'eureka'*, but in its modest way it was a revelation. I realised that parting with Hardwick Hall must be the solution. I put the idea to Dugald and he approved. As a result, my ancestor Bess of Hardwick's mansion, its contents and 3,000 acres of farmland surrounding it were transferred to the Treasury, who in turn passed it on to the National Trust. My grandmother, who had always preferred the house to Chatsworth, continued to live there until she died in 1960 and she was in her element at Hardwick, particularly in the restoration of the tapestries.

The loss of many family assets resulting from my father's death remains a sadness. I don't feel the same about Hardwick. It is unlikely that we would have found a tenant after my grandmother died and I suspect I would have approached the Trust to see whether they were interested in acquiring the property. As it was, they proved to be admirable owners. In the intervening years they have refaced much of the stonework and made great improvements to the garden. No praise is too high for the way they have looked after Hardwick Hall.

Parallel to coping with the demands of death duties ran the ques-tion of where we should live with our young family. At the time of my father's death we were living in Edensor House, in the park, previously the chief agent's house. It faced north and east and was not particularly nice. We had two children then and after allowing for nursery accommodation there was just enough room to have three people to stay. We would often drive from Edensor over Paine's beautiful bridge and gaze at Chatsworth. Debo would say 'That's a lovely house. I wonder who lives there.'

It was Bess of Hardwick who chose the site for her Elizabethan house, nothing of which survives today. The main block of Chatsworth was built on that site, dominating the park. It looks its best in evening sunlight, with a calm opulence about the west front – architecturally the best – with its gilded window frames. The house's presence so close to us and the fact that it had lain empty now for more than ten years began to dominate our thinking. Did we really have to abandon it as a family after more than 250 years of occupation?

Debo was anxious that we should move into some part of it. Hugo Read, the chief agent in Derbyshire and a man of vision, was on her side. My financial advisers had to offer caution because although we would not live in the whole of the house the operation of moving was bound to be expensive. In the end I decided that I was more frightened of my wife than my advisers; so the decision was taken to return. The credit must go to Debo for being the moving spirit behind one of the most fortunate events of my life.

We knew the move would be an expensive undertaking. I had to decide what further works of art would have to be sold to pay for the renovation and redecoration of our rooms, which among other things involved the installation of seventeen new bathrooms. The work itself took more than two years. By this time Chatsworth was open to the public four days a week – and the garden every day – from April to October. However, when deciding on which rooms the public should see and what route they should take round the house, the possibility of my family returning to live there had been borne in mind. In particular, the south-facing rooms on the first floor and most of the rooms on the west side of the house including the West Front Hall were excluded from the public route. This turned out to be a fortunate decision. In opening a house to the public it is always possible to put further rooms on view, but difficult, once established, to reduce the public access.

We would continue to pay the death duties arising from my

father's death but, thanks to the skill shown by Dugald Macpherson and his partners at Currey & Co, the light at the end of this particular tunnel was beginning to show. Furthermore there was by now a Conservative Government. The Treasury wrangles lasted seventeen years and it was twenty-four years before the whole debt and resulting interest were finally paid off. Hardwick – then the largest deal between a private family and the Treasury – was valued at £1.2m. The eight greatest works of art taken from the collection had by now so appreciated in value, partly in real terms and partly because of inflation, that they represented four-fifths of the value of the whole collection at the time of my father's death. The fact that this was, at least in part, foreseen underpinned the strategy of extending negotiations. Certainly it was our salvation. We began to look like the one that got away. Compton Place was leased, and still is, as a school and the 120,000 acres my father had owned were reduced to 72,000. There was an unexpected benefit in that the management of the various estates was streamlined and the number of estate offices and agents reduced to a base at Chatsworth.

On 7 November 1959 I returned to Chatsworth. Debo had moved in a few days earlier, as I had had to be in London, and now she herself had to be away; so I was there alone, except for our two-year-old daughter Sophy, as my son and elder daughter were at school.

I can remember sitting on the big red sofa in the drawing room. A bright fire was burning. My heart was full. The house had not been lived in by my family for twenty years and, since the departure of Penrhos College (the school which occupied it during the war) it had been virtually empty, except for a couple of house-maids, for thirteen years. It had been a long haul getting the house habitable again, and I hadn't at that stage formulated the plan of setting up the House Trust that would address the financial problems of its continuing upkeep, but the realisation that the Cavendishes were back at Chatsworth was very sweet.

Debo had done up the part of the house in which we were to live quite beautifully. At the first house party we had a few weeks later she was paid a fitting tribute by Nancy Lancaster, one of the guests and herself a well-known decorator. After she had seen all that Debo had done she turned to me and said, 'My God, you're lucky, Andrew. If I had done this house for you, you would have had to sell it to pay me.'

Public Preoccupations

Ⓢ

In the winter of 1951 I was approached by representatives of the then Buxton Borough Council to ask if I would consider becoming the next mayor. I was flattered and a little surprised. There was a time, in my father's day, when you half expected to be asked to be King of Albania, but I'd always thought the Buxton mayoralty less haphazard, more the reward for application in the council chamber. It was arranged that I should meet the current mayor and see if matters could be carried forward. He turned out to be a very nice solicitor called Henry Hartley, who was a supporter of the Labour Party.

Henry explained that there was a gap in the council between those who had been aldermen or councillors prior to the war and the newer, younger members elected since 1945. The council's view was that it would be as well to have an outsider as mayor while the younger generation of councillors found their feet. Henry seemed to think I might pass muster, so I accepted.

My family's connection with Buxton goes back a long way. When Mary Queen of Scots was imprisoned at Chatsworth (as a result of Bess of Hardwick's marriage to the Earl of Shrewsbury, Mary's custodian), the poor lady used to take the spa waters there. Later the 5th Duke of Devonshire (1748–1811) employed Carr of York to build The Crescent and its stables, for many years the Devonshire Royal Hospital and now part of the University of Derby. My own connection was less exotic, but I am still a frequent visitor to the town, and I made a lot of friends.

In those days mayor-making took place in November, marked by a procession from the Town Hall to the parish church. Understandably, Debo was not too keen on being mayoress: the prospect of going to numerous church fêtes, meetings of the Mothers' Union and endless other local commitments did not appeal to her. However, she gamely agreed to give it a shot.

The day dawned. As the procession assembled, I was very conscious that Debo was putting on a brave face. Buxton can be forbidding in November. On this particular day, though it was dry, there were black clouds overhead. The mace bearer, who led the way, was called Light, so I couldn't resist getting the procession on the move by calling out 'Lead, kindly Light, amidst the encircling gloom.'

My first council meeting was like a Saki short story. The main item on the agenda was whether the corporation-owned Pavilion Gardens, which contained a restaurant, reception hall, cafeteria and conservatory as well as gardens, should become permanently licensed premises rather than having the occasional special licence. Prior to the council meeting, the town clerk had warned me that the council was deeply divided on the issue. It cut across party lines and was between those councillors representing the Methodist vote and those who looked to the wider interests of the town. He told me that if matters got out of hand I should stand up, upon which the members of council would be obliged to defer to me, or – put more succinctly – shut up.

The meeting started at 7.30 pm. By 11.30 the debate had become heated. Two aldermen got involved in an argument. Neither would give way. Remembering the town clerk's advice I rose to my feet. Neither of them sat down, but both were so incensed by my interference that they stormed out of the chamber. So the outcome was equally salutary, if not as exactly foreseen. After this the discussion continued in a calmer atmosphere. The debate concluded at 1.30 am. A vote was called for and to my dismay the result was a tie. I would have to give the casting vote. I felt that as the council was equally divided I should come down in favour of no change. With the result that the Pavilion Gardens remained unlicensed.

I think it was the right decision, but it had its anomalous side. As word got round that my vote had been against granting a full licence to the Gardens, I became, incongruously, the hero of the teetotallers in the borough. I found myself invited to endless gatherings at which tea, coffee or soft drinks were the order of the day. Driving home after such events I wondered how some of my London friends would react to the news that I was the local champion of the teetotal cause.

I enjoyed my first year as mayor of Buxton. Debo was noble and did more than was required of her. For my part I learnt lessons that would serve me well in later years. I realised that in any corporate body there are those whom you can trust to do what they say they will do and there are the broken reeds who will let you down. I became aware, too, of the need for patience, the need to allow people time to express their views. They must be left feeling they have had a fair hearing.

Much of a mayor's work is social. Even in a small borough like Buxton, now merely part of the High Peak Borough Council, the social demands were heavy – between four and five evenings a week, except during the national holidays. First and foremost I had to appear to be enjoying myself. Often I was, but not always, and then I had to remind myself that my presence as mayor was to endorse the efforts of the organisers, and that particular event was likely to be the big day of their year. To appear bored or to leave early could cause hurt feelings. Having said that, I'm sure there were occasions when I fell short of these principles and woke the next morning full of regret.

There was the odd agreeable surprise. I remember complaining to Debo that I had to attend the annual dinner of the Licensed Victuallers' Association. But then, after the inevitable sweet sherry reception, I found myself seated at dinner next to a licensee called George Ludlow. Before the First World War he had been valet to one of the major American art collectors. As a result he had had frequent contact with the famous art collector and dealer, Joseph Duveen. Indeed Duveen used Ludlow as a go-between, ringing him up to find out what sort of temper the American employer was in, and always tipping him $15 when he came round.

Ludlow told me how on one occasion his employer had been in

Europe on his own, buying pictures without Duveen's advice. He returned with a Rubens. Duveen came round to see it and pronounced it a fake; whereupon Ludlow was sent for and ordered to take the picture to the attic.

Some time later the art collector's son announced his engagement. Father and son didn't get on. Ludlow was summoned, reminded of the picture, and told to take it to a restorer. When it came back the collector gave his son the pseudo-Rubens as a wedding present.

On another occasion, when the American returned to New York after another trip buying pictures without Duveen's advice, Duveen rang up and asked Ludlow what had been purchased. Ludlow wasn't able to help. Duveen said that all he required of Ludlow was a description of the frames and he would know the pictures.

I was asked, and accepted, to serve a second year as mayor. I made it a condition that not so many demands should be made on Debo and, to a lesser extent, on my time. Nevertheless, it was a mistake. Second helpings are seldom as good as the first. I lost some of my enthusiasm. I also knew which particular events were likely to be dull. The temptation to find excuses for not attending was often irresistible. But I ran my course and the connection came formally to an end in November 1954.

In the '50s I was not entirely preoccupied with the settlement of death duties. On the sporting side, I was a regular racegoer and I was appointed Chairman of the Lawn Tennis Association. This turned out to be a mistake. I used to love Wimbledon, but a pleasure that becomes a duty soon loses its charm. I was expected to go at least four days in each of the two weeks. The position also involved tact. Although the LTA is the governing body of lawn tennis in the UK, Wimbledon is organised by the All England Lawn Tennis and Croquet Club. In those days, before Wimbledon became part of the professional game after the 1967 championships, there was a certain Corinthian hauteur among the All England committee members. I had the feeling that they regarded themselves as superior to their counterparts on the LTA, with the inevitable resulting friction. The Davis and Wightman Cups and the National Hard Court Championships were entirely the responsibility of the LTA. I was expected to attend these events and Davis Cup matches sometimes meant travelling at weekends, which was not something I wanted to do.

When I resigned, on joining the Government in 1960, it was with relief. Although during my years as president of the LTA my relationship with the All England Club was at times not altogether easy, the club treated me most handsomely in electing me a vice-president. This is an ideal position – no work or responsibility but valuable perks: two seats in the Royal Box on request and the right to two seats on Centre Court and No. 1 Court for the fortnight. The latter is invaluable and many friends love to go.

After my political chapter closed in 1964, I became a Steward of the Jockey Club for three years and thereafter considerably extended my involvement with charities. I became Chairman (for twenty-five years) of the Cancer Research Campaign, President of the Royal National Institute for the Blind, President of the National Deaf Children's Society, President of the Royal Hospital and Home, Putney (now the Royal Hospital for Neuro-Disability), and locally Mencap and many others. In my capacity as President of the Derbyshire Scouts I received a letter from an unworldly clergyman beginning 'Knowing as I do of your keen interest in Boy Scouts ...'

Victorian grandees indulged conspicuously in charitable building, from hospitals and institutions to schools and almshouses. There may have been a degree of self-commemoration – a pat on the head for the less fortunate by the fortunate makes clear which is the taller – but in the main it was reconciling the benefits of position with what they perceived as its obligations. Nowadays, with fund-raising largely in the hands of professionals, we cope, selectively, with the non-stop assault on both our generosity and our conscience by parting with easily manageable amounts and not thinking much about the benefits we may or may not be conferring. The fund-raisers have no quibble with that; they are interested in receipts not motives. But the giving of your time is much more complex and often a much more two-way affair. The run of the mill activities of charitable work – bring and buy sales, coffee mornings, meetings in each other's houses to discuss specific projects – give an added dimension to the lives of those involved. They feel they are helping others, but at the same time they generate for themselves a feeling of belonging. Looking at charitable work as a whole, I believe at least as much benefit accrues to those working for the charity as to those for whom they are working. The need for belonging is a very real one.

I found this particularly true of my time with Barnardo's. 1986 marked their 'Year of the Volunteer', with functions up and down the country. We had a garden party at Chatsworth for 8,000 people, where the late Princess of Wales was a resounding success. I saw her twice, too, on visits to the Putney hospital. It was on such occasions that she was at her best. The patients she talked to were completely won over.

I well remember my first visit to the hospital at Putney. I had been dreading it and yet I had only entered the hall to feel this extraordinarily happy atmosphere. The patients there mostly suffered from strokes, multiple sclerosis or acute rheumatism. They were virtually all in wheelchairs and a considerable number had to lie permanently flat on their backs. Many patients also had a degree of mental handicap. If ever there was a way to set one's own petty problems into proportion, a visit to Putney could not have been more salutary.

The hospital (which had 385 beds) also had an annexe on the outskirts of Brighton, with forty beds, and I was down there one day talking to the marvellous man who ran it. I said 'In a relatively small community such as this, there must occasionally be rows.' He laughed and said 'Indeed there are. Mr Brown will complain that Mrs Smith had two slices of cake, while he had only one.' He then said 'But I have never heard anyone complain of their disablement.' The same was true at Putney.

The hospital was administered by a Board of Governors and the staff supported by a host of voluntary workers who fulfilled a number of different roles. Some manned the hospital shop, others took control of social activities, but perhaps the most important were the voluntary visitors to the hospital, each of whom had a regular group of patients they visited once or twice a week. These visits added enormously to the lives of the residents.

The work of the Cancer Research Campaign was another fine example of a great charitable organisation. Its income in 1946 was £126,000. In 2002 the Campaign merged with the Imperial Cancer Research Fund to form Cancer Research UK. Their income in 2002/3 was £270 million. Even allowing for inflation, it is a remarkable increase. Fund-raising for cancer is of course a relatively easy cause since the scourge of the disease touches virtually everyone in the UK. People who have suffered personal tragedy through the loss of a loved one are only too ready to give to an organisation which is working towards finding a cure. We found that the cost of fund-raising as a proportion of receipts shrunk eventually to as little as 5p in the pound. Some years ago, by contrast, I was associated with an organisation for the welfare of mentally handicapped ex-servicemen. The number of sufferers was fairly small and the organisation was finding it had to spend about 80p to raise a pound.

I also had the good fortune to be associated with the National Deaf Children's Society and the RNIB. It is rare for any child to suffer from just one handicap. Children born deaf are speech-impaired because they cannot hear. Equally children born blind all too often, but not always, have another handicap, usually mental. It is the children with more than one handicap who really pose the problem.

I was influenced in becoming involved with mentally handi-capped children by seeing a film called *Stress*, made in the '60s. It showed graphically the problems facing the parents of such children and it made a lasting impression on me. I became President of the East Midlands region of the Society for Mentally Handi-capped Children and Adults, MENCAP. The society has grown immensely since the war and those who work for it are among the most dedicated people I have met. Jackie Tunnicliffe, who runs the Matlock branch, is an inspiration. A high proportion of those concerned have personal experience of the problems. Much has been done in setting up special schools and in creating local branches. It is a good example of how a problem shared becomes lighter. At local meetings parents of handicapped children and those associated with adults suffering from a similar handicap meet and find that they have the same problems to bear and this makes things easier.

In the early days it appalled me that all too often there was a sense of shame at being the parent of a mentally handicapped child. I think that the Society has helped to eradicate this. Meanwhile techniques for helping the educationally subnormal are being improved and the feasibility of involving educationally subnormal children in the same classroom as those with no mental handicap is being addressed.

Politics

I was determined to stand for Parliament in 1945. West Derbyshire, my father's old constituency, was no longer an option. In February 1944 my brother had contested the by-election there after Henry Hunloke, my father's brother-in-law and the then Member, had been posted to the Middle East and decided to resign his seat. In using his influence to have Billy chosen as candidate for West Derbyshire, my father showed an unusual lack of judgement. He was accused, with some justification, of treating the constituency as a 'rotten borough'. His bitter political rival, Charlie White, stood against Billy and beat him convincingly. But in the General Election the following year, with its huge swing to Labour, he only held the seat by 156 votes and in 1950 it fell to the Conservatives.

I realised I did not have the qualifications for getting a winnable seat, so I tried to get adopted for constituencies in the East End of London. I was unsuccessful there, so I next tried North East Derbyshire – for which latterly the 'Beast of Bolsover', Dennis Skinner, has been the long-serving Member. Again I was unsuccessful, but I had a stroke of luck in that the Chairman of the Chesterfield Conservative Association was on the selection committee and approached me after the interview to ask if I would consider standing for Chesterfield. I was naturally delighted and in due course I was adopted.

The constituents, however approachable as townspeople, were unlikely to propel me into the House of Commons – Chesterfield had only been held by a Conservative after the landslide General Election of 1931. But Debo and I threw ourselves into the campaign. It was rough. We were tripped up, spat upon and on one occasion a hostile crowd tried to overturn our car. For all that, it was an experience I should have been extremely sorry to miss.

With often three meetings a night, most of which were well attended, I came face to face with a significant proportion of the electorate. I learnt how to deal with awkward questions. It is difficult to frame a question so tightly that you box in your opponent, whereas it is relatively easy to turn a question so that you reply in the manner of your choice and to your seeming advantage. We had to put up with a lot of heckling, which again was a challenge but enjoyable. There was one engagingly forthright man who expressed very strong left-wing views, though I doubt if he was as extreme as he pretended. He used to follow us round from meeting to meeting and by the end of the campaign we had become rather incongruous friends.

Canvassing was exhausting. Debo tried it once and said 'Never again.' I never expected to win, but in a campaign you are surrounded by your supporters and you get a distorted view of how you are doing. I had enthusiastic workers who distributed my election address and helped with the various promotional chores. On polling day we drove round to all the many polling stations and at about 5 pm I realised just what I was up against. As the factories closed, thousands of people appeared on the streets on their way to vote. Any fool could see they were not going to vote for me.

Owing to the time needed to receive votes from servicemen abroad, there was a delay of two weeks before the count. This was welcome. I had got leave from my regiment to contest the election and I was allowed to be away until after the declaration of the poll. Debo and I spent a happy fortnight together.

The count took place in Chesterfield Market Hall. Though we arrived early, counting had already started. It was clear at once that I was going to lose heavily. I was not depressed, I had expected it. I was amused when the town clerk as returning officer drew my attention on a fair number of occasions to ballot papers with crosses marked in favour of George Benson, my opponent, but with additions, frequently in four letter words, about me. A voter should only put a cross against the name of the candidate for whom he wishes to vote. Anything in addition is technically counted as a spoilt paper and is not included. The returning officer would ask me 'Are you prepared to let this vote stand?' Technically I could have objected, but it was only too clear what the voter had intended, so I was ready to agree.

After about four hours the count was completed. All the candidates and their wives went on to the balcony to hear the returning officer announce the result. I had been beaten by over 12,000 votes. I was disappointed by the size of the majority. Later it transpired that I had not done too badly: in fact I had reduced the Labour majority from the previous General Election by something over 2,000 votes. In an election where Labour won a landslide victory this was a rare reversal of the national trend.

In the years that followed I tried to get adopted for a safe seat, but with no success. I got onto a number of short lists, but without being selected, and it wasn't always a happy experience. On one occasion the six candidates and their wives were all herded into one room to wait to be interviewed in turn by the committee. Conversation wasn't easy when we were all strangers competing for the same job. I remember driving away having failed to get the nomination of Woking, and thinking 'That's it.' If there was a healthy lesson to be learned, it was that no amount of privilege could acquire me a safe Tory seat. So I returned to Chesterfield, where I worked hard at nursing the constituency ahead of the next General Election, which took place in 1950.

The campaign was less stormy than that of 1945. The constituency boundaries had been redrawn, to include the industrial town of Staveley, which was even more solidly Labour. It was no surprise that I was beaten by a majority of nearly 17,000 votes. The result looked very bad unless you were aware of the boundary changes. Since the name of the constituency made no mention of Staveley and nationally there had been a major swing back to the Tories, to be beaten in 1945 by 12,000 votes and then in 1950 by nearly 17,000 made sorry reading.

The 1950 election ended my attempts to get into the House of Commons. At the time I was disappointed, but looking back I am not sorry. My father died later that year and in those days it was not possible to renounce your title. I had no option but to go to the House of Lords. When legislation was passed to make renouncing possible, friends asked me if I was considering it. I would answer 'If you look at the figures for the two campaigns I fought you will understand when I say "Not likely."' I was going to stick to the warmth and safety of Their Lordships' House.

The Suez crisis of 1956 saw my maiden speech in the House of Lords. I fervently supported the Government's policy of military intervention. It so happened that in the early days of the crisis I spoke at the annual dinner of the Royal Society of St George, of which I was President. In my speech I spoke strongly in favour of the joint Anglo-French action. David Maxwell Fyfe, later Lord Kilmuir and a member of the Government, was a guest. He was kind enough afterwards to congratulate me on my speech and encouraged me to express similar views in the forthcoming debate in the Lords.

I looked at Suez in the context of Munich. The latter had left a deep scar on the Tory conscience. Many of those who had supported Mr Chamberlain came to realise that while in practical terms the Munich agreement may have been the right decision, morally it was deeply shaming. It coloured Conservative opinion at the time of Suez. Nasser, wrongly, was equated with Hitler and the Government should not give in to him: yet another dictator who broke his word and tore up treaties. Many leading supporters of Munich became chief advocates of the Government's action over the annexation of the Suez Canal. I was with them entirely.

Whatever the virtues of the decision, no one could admire the way it was handled. If you are going to stage a coup to overthrow a government, speed is of the essence. Day after day went by while our invasion force sailed from Malta to Port Said. Meanwhile those opposed to the venture worked up a head of steam against what they saw as an act of atrocious British colonialism.

A maiden speech is not the easiest of occasions. It is far better to make your first speech in a low key and on an uncontroversial issue. I was in a highly emotional state over the whole thing and could not keep silent. It is the convention in the Upper House that on the occasion of his first speech a peer should be allowed to speak early in the debate. I followed the Labour Front Bench spokesman, Lord Jowitt, who understandably expressed his party's opposition to Britain's intervention at length. He was on his feet for over an hour. Increasingly nervous, I sat as the distinguished former Lord Chancellor went on and on and on.

Finally he came to his peroration and sat down. It was my turn. I rose with trepidation. I have no idea what sort of speech I made and I never had the courage to read it afterwards. But the House of Lords was a tolerant audience, particularly when the speaker was a newcomer. Their Lordships were singularly kind to me and I sat down reasonably satisfied.

There was, however, a second convention applicable to a maiden speech. The peer should not leave the Chamber until the speaker following him had sat down. Leslie Hore-Belisha followed me. With less justification than Lord Jowitt, he too spoke for over an hour, starting about 7 pm. I felt badly in need of a drink but I had to sit through Leslie's seemingly unending discourse until I got it. The speech was sad and, ironically, his swan song. Very soon after he had a heart attack and died.

The after-effects of Suez were many and far-reaching. The most immediate and important was the resignation of Anthony Eden. Bad health was the official reason for this, and I don't subscribe to the suggestion that it was a diplomatic illness and that he had felt obliged to resign owing to the failure of his Government's policy, for which as Prime Minister he was ultimately responsible. From my point of view, the nomination of Harold Macmillan as his successor was to be an unmitigated boon. In the years that followed I was singled out for special favour. It was entirely due to Uncle Harold's influence that I was able to embark on my modest and short-lived political career. The word 'nepotism' could never have been better applied. I felt – and still feel – a debt of gratitude I could never repay.

The author (left) with his parents and brother Billy, Churchdale, 1923

LEFT The author, 1928 RIGHT His parents with Elizabeth (left) and Anne, Churchdale, 1930

The 9th Duke and seventeen of his grandchildren, Christmas 1931 (author 3rd from right)

ABOVE Hardwick Hall BELOW Chatsworth

ABOVE Wedding, 1941: Debo's parents, Lord and Lady Redesdale (third from left and extreme left), with author's parents and Billy BELOW Going away: Arbell Mackintosh (author's cousin) and Henry Wyndham

ABOVE Billy's marriage to Kick Kennedy. Joseph Kennedy, behind the bride, the eldest Kennedy son, was killed in a flying accident later that year (1944).
BELOW, RIGHT Election address photograph, 1945

MISS KATHLEEN KENNEDY —whom we must now think of as Lady Hartington—is returning to London next week from her honeymoon. I understand that she is to go back to her job at the U.S. Red Cross Club in Hans - crescent, Knightsbridge, where she acts as a hostess for American troops.

Cables flashing across the Atlantic last week between the Devonshire family and Mr. Joseph Kennedy, former U.S. Ambassador in London, whose daughter has married the Marquis of Hartington, the Duke of Devonshire's heir, have settled, at any rate for the time being, the religious question raised

It has been agreed that any children shall not be brought up in the Catholic faith of the Kennedys, and accordingly, no religious ceremony will follow the civil marriage.

July 1945: author and Debo with Emma and Peregrine and dogs Johnny and Bengy

The author on the pump in the Market Square, Chesterfield, in the 1950 election

J. W. O'Neill (Lib), the author (Con), G. Benson (Soc), B. Barker (Comm)

BARBERS, greengrocers, cobblers, and chip shop proprietors along Chatsworth-road here today talked politics with a duke's son.

Lord Hartington, 31-year-old Conservative and National Liberal candidate in the four-cornered Chesterfield fight, was grateful to find many of them willing to display his large election picture in their windows.

"It looks as though I've got a black eye," he said. "But otherwise it's not a bad likeness." A greengrocer's wife told him : "I nearly got a black eye for sticking up for you at the last election."

Replied 6ft. 2½in. Lord Hartington : "If that happens again, just send for me."

When the son of Chesterfield's lord of the manor strode into the Co-op. grocery shop assistants grinned. They laughed outright when Lord Hartington asked them to put up his picture, but they said they would read his Tory leaflets.

On the other side of the street Lady Hartington, the candidate's good-looking wife, was rapidly making her husband Chatsworth-road's pin-up man.

She handed out nearly 50 poster photographs. One old man stopped her, shook hands, and told her he had voted for her husband's great-grandfather nearly 60 years ago.

Lady Hartington fitted in a little urgent shopping. She explained: "The children are both ill with chickenpox. It would have to happen at election time."

Lord Hartington is the hardest worker of the four candidates. So far, the Socialists, confident of an increased majority, have kept aloof from the fray. Their candidate, Mr. George Benson, opens his campaign tomorrow night.

MYSTERY

The Liberals whose candidate is Mr. John O'Neill, 40-year-old assistant manager of a Sheffield store, are something of a mystery

Little has been heard, either, of the Communist, Mr. Basil Barker, who lived from 1935 to 1937 in the Soviet Union.

ABOVE Lismore BELOW Adele Astaire with her second husband, Kingman Douglass, 1947

Harold Macmillan was married to my father's sister Dorothy. I saw him from time to time on family occasions during my schooldays – he was one of the few with whom my grandfather seemed to be at ease even after his stroke – and when he came to Chatsworth for Christmas. There was an affinity between us. My mother was a constant comfort to him over Dorothy's much-publicised romance with Bob Boothby and possibly his gratitude to her for that prompted many of the kindnesses he showed to me. Yet I have always wondered whether his urge to dispense favours stemmed from a feeling that neither the Cavendish or Cecil families quite regarded him as one of them; and showing he could bestow patronage on their children was his response. Even so, I like to think he was too shrewd an operator to risk employing people, particularly relations, who weren't up to the job. Lady Harlech was my mother's sister and the mother of David, whose appointment first as Minister of State in the Foreign Office and then as our Ambassador in Washington was achieved entirely on merit. Julian Amery, Uncle Harold's son-in-law, also deserved his Government post. Julian, if rather right wing for my taste, was a clever and able politician. However, my appointment as Under-Secretary of State in the Commonwealth Office was rightly acknowledged as a stupendous act of nepotism. I consoled myself with the belief that Uncle Harold must have been reasonably confident that I wouldn't let him down.

To use an unkind literary analogy, Uncle Harold would like to have been thought of as a Trollopian character whereas in fact he was straight out of Galsworthy. He could be extremely good company, and he had the most beautiful manners. He was courtesy itself. Like so many of his generation he was deeply affected by his experiences in the First World War. He was badly wounded in the leg, but managed in some extraordinary way to reach safety. He told me that, while he had loved his time at Oxford, he couldn't bring himself to go there for six years after the war because of its associations with so many of his contemporaries who had been killed.

He was originally on the left of the Conservative Party and it was quite an achievement to hold Stockton-on-Tees as a Tory in the years before the war. He wasn't at that time a natural with the grass roots – there was a certain aloofness, probably more shyness than arrogance – and here Aunt Dorothy, for all the matrimonial tribulations, really played her part. She had the all-important gift of being exactly the same with everybody. She was entirely without 'side'. I remember her bringing parties of constituents on day outings to Chatsworth, and she certainly fostered the constituency.

In the account of the fighting in Italy I have already touched on Uncle Harold's first practical intervention in my life in having me withdrawn to a training camp. Though kindly meant, it was something that bitterly upset me, though I never raised the matter with him in all the subsequent years we had dealings with each other.

Appointed to succeed Eden in 1957, he brought an unexpected truth to Rab Butler's slightly sour description of him as 'the best Prime Minister we have'. The voting public began to relax their uncertainty about his intellectual and aristocratic manner, and the Conservatives won the election of 1959 to give him a new term in office. Not because he had been holding his best card up his sleeve, it was only in the autumn of the following year that he took steps to involve me in an active role in politics.

He first suggested that I should become a lord-in-waiting – the lowest rung on the ladder for those with political ambitions. This I resisted. I was busy with a host of activities and happy with what I was doing. I was concerned with quite a few charities, steward at a number of race meetings, President of the Lawn Tennis Association, and in my Derbyshire life meeting the considerable demands of local affairs. On top of that, the settlement of death duties was still taking up an unwelcome proportion of my time. All in all I was unwilling to give up my way of life for a job, which, possibly essential if I was to have a political career, did not in itself amount to much.

In the event, my attitude of playing hard to get paid off. A less generous man than Uncle Harold would have written me off as a political prospect. In the autumn of 1960 I was offered the position of Parliamentary Under-Secretary of State in the Commonwealth Relations Office. The title may sound grand, but only someone who has held that office can have any conception of how unimportant it is. Having said that, in the ladder of any career there must always be a first rung. I once described the job as not being responsible for making the tea, but for doing the washing up. Nevertheless, it was better than being a lord-in-waiting. This time I was sensible to accept the offer, ill-deserved though it might have been.

I saw Uncle Harold on a Friday morning in early October at Admiralty House, then the Prime Minister's official residence as No. 10 was being restored. He was sitting up in bed at about 10.30 am. He suggested I take on the job. There was to be no announcement for ten days. I returned to Chatsworth very late that evening to find a letter from the then Senior Steward of the Jockey Club inviting me to become the junior of the then three Stewards in the following year. This meant, barring accidents, I would have become Senior Steward in three years' time. To be a Steward of the Jockey Club had been a long-standing ambition. Had I received the letter before seeing Uncle Harold, I would have accepted. Now I was committed elsewhere and had to decline. Once again, luck was on my side in that in the late '60s when the Conservatives were in opposition the Jockey Club were kind enough to renew the invitation; so I achieved my aim after all, although by then the number of Stewards had been increased to nine.

In the meantime I had four years at the Commonwealth Office, among the happiest of my life. The Secretary of State was Duncan Sandys, the Minister of State Cub Alport. Duncan was a strange man. His mind worked much in the manner of the mills of God. He was already a social acquaintance, but at my first meeting with him, in his rather daunting office overlooking the Cenotaph, he didn't go out of his way to put me at my ease. He had no hesitation in telling me that he had told Uncle Harold, when informed that I was to be his new Parliamentary Under-Secretary, that he, Duncan, thought the appointment would be very badly received.

These comments were justified but did not add to my confidence over my fitness for the job or help to establish a cordial relationship between us. I took comfort in the knowledge that whatever Duncan might think about it, I had the Prime Minister's support and at the end of the day Duncan, too, had to defer to Uncle Harold's opinion.

Uncle Harold was a consummate actor. I remember staying at his home, Birch Grove, during his Premiership and watching him walking to church with one of his contemporaries. He was being the man of property, saying more land was to be bought (gesturing) 'over there, to make a second day's shooting'. During the service he read one of the lessons and suddenly he was the old, old man bowed down by the cares of office as he struggled up the aisle to the lectern.

No recollection of Uncle Harold in office would be complete without reference to John Wyndham. John had become a good friend of mine at Cambridge, and he, Debo and I were extremely close in the years after the war. On becoming Prime Minister Uncle Harold made John one of his private secretaries and main speech writer, at which John was brilliant. I remember one occasion when Solly Zuckerman gave a great party at the London Zoo, of which he was then head. The guests included Uncle Harold as Prime Minister and Hugh Gaitskell as Leader of the Opposition. Both had to speak. Uncle Harold gave John and me a lift home. He was very pleased with his speech and said 'Well, of course, Hugh's speech was all right, but he had clearly burnt the midnight oil over it. Whereas mine came off with the lightest of touches.' John leant forward. 'Uncle Harold,' he pointed out, 'I wrote that speech.'

Shortly after my appointment there was a major debate in the Lords on the future of the Rhodesian Federation. The Government's policy was under strong criticism. Quintin Hailsham, Leader of the House, sent for me to discuss my participation in the debate, explaining that normally new Ministers were given as easy a baptism of fire as possible. For me to speak on the Rhodesian debate would hardly be that. Although he did not allude to it, he was also aware of the unusual circumstances of my recent appointment to the Government ranks. However, he saw no alternative other than for me to open for the Government and did his best to give me confidence. That meeting was the start of a lasting friendship.

Though none of my previous speeches had been of any consequence, I had made a number to a wide variety of audiences. However, other than occasionally putting down a brief note, I would speak without a script. I had never learnt to read a speech and found this much more difficult than to speak without notes. As a Government spokesman I was not speaking for myself, but for Her Majesty's Government, and had to get it right. I was compelled to stick to a prepared text and in the days prior to the debate Duncan found the time to help me prepare it. I rehearsed it again and again.

In the event it passed off reasonably well. It was platitudinous and dull. When it was over, Duncan, who had been listening from the steps of the Throne, sent me a kind congratulatory note. I think he was surprised by my performance and the speech broke the ice between us and so started a friendship which was to grow over the next four years.

Having my first official speech out of the way was an enormous relief. I walked back from Westminster to my house in Chesterfield Street feeling ten years younger and regretting my inability to whistle. Early the next morning Uncle Harold rang to say that he had heard all had gone smoothly, for which no doubt he was as relieved as I was.

Duncan was difficult. Commonwealth diplomats and civil servants would call in on me, either before or after seeing him, seeking advice as to how best to get his approval and on occasion for solace after having a rough time with him. One of the problems of interviews with him was that you went in to discuss a Caribbean issue, for example, and then he would turn to a totally different subject and get cross if you were not briefed on it.

For much of the time we worked together he was unmarried and lived in Vincent Square, quite close to the Commons. He was a workaholic and liked to call conferences at 6 pm on Fridays. This was all very well for him, but, as I liked to spend the weekends at Chatsworth and often had guests, it could prove tiresome as these conferences frequently went on until near midnight. One could have a glass of whisky but, as a fellow Minister put it to me after one such occasion, not nearly enough.

I may have served a useful purpose in the Office in smoothing Duncan's abrasive edges. Working with him was an experience. He disliked reading papers, preferring to have the problem explained verbally. This took time and I frequently became impatient that he would never take the point, only to find at the end of the discussion that he came up with a pertinent detail which I had missed.

I recollect a row with the Treasury over how much the CRO could spend on information services. Before the preliminary meeting, which I was to attend, Duncan told me to resist all Treasury demands for cuts. This I did, the matter then being referred to a meeting between the Foreign Secretary, Duncan and some officials from the Chancellor's Office. I was allowed to go along. As soon as the Treasury raised their objections Duncan gave way. I was so angry that I left the room. The next morning Duncan, rather than sending for me, came to my room to apologise.

In the main, however, I admired Duncan. He liked power. I remember attending a meeting when it was to be decided whether British troops should be sent in during the series of mutinies in Kenya, Tanzania and Uganda. Duncan had a senior military officer present and decided on ordering troops into action. The general pointed out that he only had to give an order over the telephone and troops would be on their way in ten minutes. 'Splendid!' said Duncan. When I piped up in a nervous squeaky voice, 'Secretary of State, should we first consult the Prime Minister?' Duncan looked at me and said, 'Oh, don't spoil it all, Andrew.' However, the Prime Minister was consulted.

I suspect Duncan was a sad man, in that he must have realised that whatever the result of the forthcoming 1964 election he was at the end of his career. Secretary of State for Commonwealth

Relations was due to be abolished as an individual office and he was unlikely to get another job even if the Tories won.

Once I had got the hang of things I enjoyed my job enormously. It was a fascinating time in the Commonwealth because the breaking up of the British Empire was entering its final stages. The modern Commonwealth was coming into existence. Originally the CRO consisted of the old Dominion Countries – Canada, Australia, New Zealand and South Africa. Then with the independence of India and Pakistan in 1947 the modern, multi-racial Commonwealth was created. My job involved a lot of travel and some of my experiences overseas are the subject of the next vignette.

The 1962 grouse season was extremely good and Uncle Harold enjoyed himself immensely with us at Bolton Abbey. By suspicious coincidence I was promoted to Minister of State that autumn. This had the bonus of a Government car and within the Office I was given access to a higher echelon of classified information. I was interested to note that when given the list of those receiving similar information, my private secretary was already on the list. It also meant that when the Secretary of State was away I was in charge of the Office.

During one such period I attended Cabinet meetings for those items on the agenda that concerned the Office. In theory such attendance only meant you were to be present for those items, but with an extension of his nepotism Uncle Harold usually allowed me to stay on for the rest of business. I cannot pretend I attended any meetings at which momentous decisions were taken. Nevertheless it was fascinating to see the Cabinet at work. I noticed that a number of members brought papers with them that had nothing to do with the agenda and would study them while matters that did not concern or interest them were being discussed.

It had its problems, in that, being a junior Minister, you naturally had to keep in the background but also try to make sure the Office's point of view was firmly represented. It was a question of timing as to when you should chip in without appearing above your station.

Two episodes on the security side remain in my memory. The first was when I was told that a very high-ranking agent of the Office was to come to see me. He duly arrived with a purple despatch box. This was new to me – members of Government had red ones, civil servants black ones. He unlocked the box and produced a large manila envelope which he handed to me. At the time President Nkrumah of Ghana was being very difficult. Inside was a letter from a European psychiatrist whom Nkrumah used to visit. The contents of the letter were to the effect that Nkrumah was getting increasingly worried about his virility. This affected his attitude to Britain: when his virility was weak he became anti-British, but if things in that area improved he swung back to being supportive of us and the Commonwealth. It went on to say that in view of the President's general health the likelihood was that his virility would continue to decline and upsurges in it would become increasingly rare. The psychiatrist advised Her Majesty's Government to draw their own conclusions.

My other recollection remains a mystery. I was told that a high-level man from MI5 or MI6 was coming to see me. The meeting took the form of a *tour d'horizon* over the whole Commonwealth scene. He was well informed and had very good manners. He asked me for my view of some aspects of Commonwealth affairs. I enjoyed the talk and it helped clear my mind over certain issues. But the purpose of the visit remains a puzzle. Looking back on it, I cannot imagine why I didn't ask him straight out. My guess is that my visitor was out to discover whether or not I had certain information.

In the early autumn of 1963 Uncle Harold underwent a major operation. His own doctor, a close friend, was away at the time. Deep depression can often follow surgery and perhaps because of it Uncle Harold decided to resign. He had few intimates. The man probably closest to him was John Wyndham, but John was young enough to be Uncle Harold's son and whatever he thought about the resignation he did not carry enough clout to persuade Uncle Harold to change his mind. So far as I know, Uncle Harold sought no advice before taking his decision. It was an unlucky coincidence that his doctor was away as it might have been a different story. He could and probably would have advised Uncle Harold to put off the decision for a few weeks. The country was not in a state of crisis and government could have continued perfectly well until the Prime Minister recovered. Churchill, after all, had continued in office in spite of a serious illness.

It resulted in the Conservatives losing the 1964 General Election. In saying this I have no wish to denigrate Alec Douglas-Home. Other than being probably too nice and unambitious a man to hold the office, he proved to be a capable Prime Minister in the run up to the election. There was not enough time for him to stamp his personality on the electorate. Uncle Harold had been the established leader of the party. Since Labour won by only a handful of seats, it is reasonable to assume that without the change the Tories would have won, albeit by a small but working majority.

I took a modest part in the election campaign, Central Office sending me to constituencies which it considered neither winnable nor losable. In the latter case they were wrong. I spoke at the eve of poll rally at one of the two Brighton seats, held in the Pavilion, and with the possible exception of some meetings in Chesterfield in 1945 it was the rowdiest I have spoken at. The noise was deafening. The greater part of the audience were from Sussex University, then conspicuous for left-wing views. I enjoyed it immensely. It was, however, a disaster for David James, the sitting Member for Kemp Town. At the declaration of the poll he was beaten by a handful of votes, the first and only seat lost to Labour in solid Tory Sussex. You can make a case for my having helped it happen.

The fall of the Government in 1964 marked the end of my brief political career. While I very much enjoyed it, I cannot claim to have achieved anything. Indeed to the best of my recollection my only contribution was a negative one. This was to persuade the Tanzanian Minister of Finance, the delightful Paul Boumani, to accept with good grace £6 million of Government aid rather than the £7 million he had been seeking. For this I got a very civil letter from John Boyd-Carpenter, then Chief Secretary to the Treasury. Whether this success was in the best interests of the Commonwealth is a different matter.

Quintin Hailsham was made Leader of the Opposition in the House of Lords. Peter Carrington was chief spokesman on Foreign Affairs and I was given the job as his number two. It was not an arduous job, although being on the Front Bench meant regular attendance at the House. Preparing a speech was hard work with no civil servants to do the devilling. I remember winding up a Foreign Affairs debate when my speech took eight hours to write, twenty-five minutes to deliver, and received two lines in the *Times* Parliamentary report, one of which was my name.

In 1966 there was a reshuffle of the Front Bench in the House of Lords, in which I became spokesman for transport. A curious assignment, since I didn't even have the qualification of having held a civil driving licence. But at least it was one of the few matters on which I could speak without giving offence. During my years as a Minister I had been aware that holding office held problems for the rich and privileged. Even in the Lords my avenues were limited by these constraints, quite apart from my own deficiencies. Foreign affairs, defence and transport were about the only portfolios available. For me to pontificate, let alone hold office, on matters of health, welfare or education would have been preposterous and, rightly, quite unacceptable to the electorate.

For example, by what right does someone living at Chatsworth lay down the law on the nation's housing problems? How can someone educated at Eton, followed there by his son and grandson, talk on behalf of his party on the state of secondary education? And what about someone who has never done a stroke of work in his life or been to a doctor other than in Harley Street, holding forth on employment or the National Health Service? It would be totally inappropriate and could only be damaging to the party to which he belongs.

I was brought up a Tory, though over the decades, indeed centuries, my family have been Whigs. I left the Conservative Party in the '80s and gave my political allegiance to the SDP. In my final days as a member of the House of Lords I sat on the cross-benches. Since being expelled from the House of Lords, following the abolition of hereditary peers, I can no longer play a part in the constitutional life of the country. As a Privy Counsellor I am entitled to sit on the steps of the Throne to listen to debates, but I am now so arthritic that if I succeeded in settling down on the steps I would have great difficulty in getting up again. I do think, however, that it would have been a reasonable acknowledgement of the honour of becoming a Privy Counsellor to have allowed those hereditary peers who were Privy Counsellors to continue to sit in the House.

Political Travels

While the principle of granting independence to the member states of the Empire had always been acknowledged, the speed of that process was a source of contention. With hindsight, in the context of the African colonies the process may have been too hurried. It is arguable, too, that the UK Government would have been wiser to build on the traditional tribal system rather than try to impose Westminster-style democracy on an insecure structure. If, in the immediate years after the war, Britain had had the support of the United States in continuing as a colonial power for a further generation and tried in that time to establish an indigenous civil service and to foster the professions and a stable middle class, the future development of the 'emerging' countries might have been less precarious. In the event, far from the United States supporting Britain in its colonial rule, they led the pack in attacking imperialism and colonialism. This was no doubt partly due to the deeply ingrained spirit of independence in the United States – once, after all, a British colony – but probably quite as persuasive to the White House were the sensitive issues involving their own coloured population, particularly in the southern states.

My appointment to the CRO involved me in extensive travelling. It was hard work, continually on the move and constantly meeting fresh faces. There was never enough time to get to know your hosts and relax. All too soon you were whisked off and the whole process of ingratiating yourself had to start all over again. I enjoyed some of the trips at the time, some were tolerable, and some I could not wait to be over. In particular I remember arriving at half past seven one morning in Winnipeg with the prospect of eight speeches to make in the next twelve hours, and saying to myself, 'What on earth are you doing here when you could be at Chatsworth going round the greenhouse?'

The speech-making was demanding. I was helped by my private secretary and I would be briefed by the High Commissioner and his staff in the relevant country. Nevertheless making speeches with political implications posed special difficulties for a junior Minister. Whereas the Secretary of State carried the full weight of the Prime Minister and Cabinet, junior Ministers were out on a limb: if they said the wrong thing Whitehall tended to declare its loyalty to the official stance in a flurry of rather dismissive telegrams to the High Commissioner.

It tended to make one blander than one would have cared to be. That was safe enough for speeches, but there was the added hazard of exchanges with the press. This difficulty was highlighted on a visit to Australia in 1962, which coincided with Britain's first negotiations for entering the European Community. The Australians regarded this as selling out the Empire to Europe. Accordingly I faced a hostile press, in any event none too keen on Poms and who regarded a ducal Pom as the last straw.

On a happier note I was particularly lucky in becoming a friend of President Kenyatta, a controversial figure because of his involvement with Mau Mau. Extreme nationalism is not intended to go down well with people on the receiving end of it, but it's a persuasive conduit to a position of authority in a country being granted independence. The colonial power has to hope for the best; and in the case of Jomo Kenyatta things could have been infinitely worse.

I am prejudiced in his favour, as he went out of his way to be nice to me. I accompanied Duncan to the celebrations for Kenya's independence. It is unusual for Heads of State to pay attention to junior Ministers. The reason for his kindness went back to 1923 when my grandfather was Secretary of State for the Colonies. At that time there was unrest among the white settlers, culminating in a march to protest at Government House. The story goes that the civil servant delegated to inform my grandfather found him playing golf. He did not, it is said, return to his office, but declared then and there 'The interests of the natives must be paramount.' If legend is to be believed, this is the foundation of what is now enshrined in Kenya's history as the 'Devonshire Declaration'. My grandfather was a good Whig and I am sure he fully understood the implications of those words. Kenyatta was very much aware of the Declaration and showed it by his outstanding courtesy to me.

At the Independence Banquet he placed me between two of his former wives. One, an Englishwoman, whom he had married in 1942 as his third wife while he was working in Sussex, had been specially flown out from England to attend the celebrations; the other was a later African wife. It was a typically African gesture, a nod both to me and the ex-wives. The discontinued marital status not only seemed to hold its value, but was dispensed as a sort of presidential largesse. Not all the often married would have used the credential so disarmingly. I doubt if one would have come up against such niceties of *place à table* dining with, say, Zsa Zsa Gabor.

During my four years eleven countries achieved independence and I attended the celebrations for five of them – Kenya, Tanganyika, Zanzibar, Uganda and Jamaica. The ceremonies all took the same form – a state banquet and receptions, then on the actual night of the granting of freedom a military tattoo, followed at midnight by the lowering of the Union Jack and the raising of the national flag. The evening would be rounded off with fireworks.

Kenya's Day of Independence was marred by torrential rain, resulting in acute traffic congestion between the city centre and the stadium where the ceremony was to be held. I managed to get through in time, but Duncan lost patience and returned to State House. In the general chaos this went unnoticed, which was, symbolically, slightly bizarre.

The following day we both attended the swearing in of Kenyatta and his senior ministers, which gave a sideline on the problem of national identity facing its leading statesmen. Whereas Tom Mboya, highly westernised, looked to be wearing a Savile Row suit, Odinga Odinga, the Vice-President, went to the other extreme, with an emphasis on national wild life in his outfit, including a monkey's tail.

When in 1965 I became Chancellor of Manchester University there came the opportunity to repay President Kenyatta's kindness. On inauguration the new Chancellor is allowed to nominate those whom he wishes to receive honorary degrees on the occasion of his installation. I included President Kenyatta in my list, the others being Dame Margot Fonteyn, Hugh Gaitskell's widow, Dora, and the late Lords Rothschild and Harlech. Only President Kenyatta regretted he was unable to attend; the rest came to Manchester for the occasion.

So later in the year I flew to Nairobi where the High Commissioner, Malcolm MacDonald, had made arrangements for the President to receive his degree. Kenyatta preferred this to take place at his farm rather than at State House. I committed a sartorial solecism by turning up in a pale suit, tie and socks, while everyone else was dressed as if for a funeral. It also rained, which caused the President to announce that the occasion was 'blessed'.

An illustration of Kenyatta's sensitivity came the following day when he gave a luncheon in my honour at State House. This time I took no chances with my clothes and arrived sombrely attired, only to find the President dressed as I had been the previous day. I have no doubt he thought I had only brought an informal wardrobe and was trying to put me at my ease.

It is difficult to analyse my feelings at the independence ceremonies. I certainly did not begrudge the people their nationhood, yet events elsewhere in the new Commonwealth were casting doubt as to what would be the effect on the welfare of the people concerned. Both at the time and with hindsight, the most poignant of the ceremonies I attended was that in Zanzibar, which followed on immediately from Kenya. It was held in the daylight but the proceedings were similar. When it was over the retiring Governor was escorted to the harbour, where a Royal Navy frigate was waiting to take him home. Duncan and I accompanied the other guests to see him off and then returned to an empty Residency; the new

President was not moving in till the following day. It was about 6 pm and as traditional Englishmen we helped ourselves to a 'sundowner', then walked out on to the terrace that overlooked the bay. The sun was setting, turning the whole sea emerald. It is known as the 'moment of green'. Around the headland came the frigate, the marine band playing on the quarterdeck as she steamed away into the sunset. An affecting epilogue to Empire.

Zanzibar's freedom, however, was short-lived and tragic. Africans, Asians and Arabs had co-existed quite harmoniously before. Within a matter of weeks the leader of the African element in the Government took over by force and atrocities followed. In the end it was merged with Tanganyika to become Tanzania. One could but ponder the old question: is it better to be well governed or govern yourself badly?

I paid a delightful visit to the Maldives. These were then a relatively little known archipelago of over a thousand coral islands stretching north and south 400 miles west of Sri Lanka. The most southerly isle, called Gan, had become an important RAF staging post for service aircraft going to the Far East. The natives of the nearby islands were growing increasingly hostile to its occupation and the purpose of my visit was a fence-mending exercise. As such it was singularly unsuccessful, but from a personal point of view I would not have missed it for anything.

I stayed with the UK's diplomatic representative. On the first night, sitting on the lawn, which stretched down to the sea, a small armada of boats rowed past, their crews shouting expletives. There was a lady among our party whose emotions were torn between shock at the language and delight that she was seeing the real world. The real world was on show again the following day with a much more serious demonstration on the quay. The authorities decided the best way to put an end to this was by turning hoses on the demonstrators. As the temperature was over 100 degrees, this merely stimulated them and did nothing to diminish their ardour. Those of us watching longed to have the hoses turned on us.

The demonstration did result in one of my few personal achievements during my years in office in that I authorised the leader of the rebellion to be banished to the Seychelles – where he apparently made a lot of money as a property developer.

I then flew to a more northerly island in the group to see the Prime Minister and the President. The PM was far from friendly, demonstrating this by making me walk the mile or so from the airstrip to his office. I was wearing a black silk suit and by the time I arrived was soaked through with sweat.

My visit to the President was happier. At least I was sent back to my aeroplane in the President's car (one of only two on the island) and our discussions were friendly enough, if inconclusive. We talked in his beautiful wooden palace consisting of a number of buildings separated by courtyards. The outsides of the buildings were painted pale blue and white, the interiors were lined with teak with highly polished floors. The courtyards were of coral sand. It was ravishing.

I then returned to London. My visit was followed by that of a senior civil servant and finally by the Secretary of State. In due course the Maldives achieved independence and have now become a popular holiday resort.

My final mission was to Malaysia and Borneo. The first stage was to accompany the then Chancellor of the Exchequer, Reggie Maudling, as his number two and represent the CRO views at an economic conference of various Commonwealth countries in the Far East, held in Malaysia. At the time the High Commissioner there, Antony Head, was an old friend. Antony had held Cabinet rank as a politician before turning his skills to diplomacy. Prior to going to Malaysia he had been High Commissioner in Nigeria. I stayed on after the end of the conference, while Reggie Maudling returned to England.

First I went to Borneo, where Communist elements were still much in evidence, though our army was present in strength. I flew by helicopter over the areas where the terrorists were thought to be. It was exciting, with soldiers sitting on the floor, legs dangling in the air and guns at the ready in case someone took a pot shot at us. The soldiers were remarkable. Admittedly they were young men, but their strength seemed to me amazing. The jungle paths I had read of turned out to be shallow, strong-running streams. It was up these the soldiers had to trudge, carrying their packs. Being interested in anything to do with the Army, I asked if I could try one on. They politely strapped one on my shoulders and I keeled over backwards. Some sort of compliment to them, I suppose, but not very dignified for me.

Social life in Borneo was in marked contrast. I attended an agricultural show which might well have been in Surrey – white elephant and cake stalls, tombola and all the rest. I went to visit a long house. I was warned that I would be offered palm wine and that it would be rude to refuse. I had not been warned of the method of offering. I sat down opposite a beautiful, topless, young lady. She duly offered the wine to me in a hefty Army-type enamel mug. I swallowed some and handed it back. She offered it to me again and I drank. She offered it a third time and I felt I had done enough both from the point of view both of manners and wine-consumption – it was strong stuff. The young lady, however, wasn't willing to take no for an answer and, having given me the mug, the process was repeated several more times. When I finally tried to call a halt, she put her arms around my neck and pressed me forward so that my face was buried in her bosom. Eventually I disentangled myself from this embrace, only to find that the routine had to be repeated several times before I got to the other end of the long house. I ended up with a very bad headache.

I stayed in a sombre grey stone house which John Piper would have loved to paint. Sleep was difficult. The Borneans are great gamblers. Their passion was cock fighting, so we were kept awake by the continuous sound of cocks crowing.

On returning to Malaysia, where incidentally the Parliament Building in Kuala Lumpur is a very fine piece of modern architecture, I was sent on a foray to the north of the country. Here I visited rubber plantations and tin mines. I also attended the equivalent of the local fête. This was a different affair from my experience in Borneo. There were demonstrations of blowpipe shooting at targets. However, one of the contestants, dissatisfied with his performance, could not resist loosing off at a passing bird. It fell to the ground. It turned out that the poison used had merely stunned it and in due course it recovered. Should it have been suitable for the pot, I doubt if it would have been so lucky.

Other attractions included boat races on narrow bamboo rafts down a fast-flowing, winding river. Again the participants' skills were remarkable. The concluding event was a beauty competition, which I was asked to judge. I accepted unwillingly, remembering my father's advice 'never to judge any competition except one for knobbly knees, because as judge you will please one person and disappoint the rest'. The contestants varied in age from eleven or twelve to ladies who appeared to be in their sixties. The only common factor was that they were all topless. I walked slowly down the line of ladies and back again. I had the sense to ask the man in charge of the occasion to whom I should award the first prize and duly did as he said. A British policeman present took some photographs, but never sent them on, which was a pity as they would have made a valuable addition to the family album.

Judging the beauty competition proved too much for me, and on returning to Government House I retired to bed feeling very ill with a high fever. I was told it was an all too familiar hazard; and though I was in bed for ten days, it might have been considerably worse. My recovery was aided by news from home that one of my horses had won a decent race – as rare an event then as it is now.

On my return to Heathrow I was met by my private secretary with a letter from the Prime Minister saying he wished me to become a member of the Privy Council. I was greatly flattered, not least because, since Alec Home was by then Prime Minister, there was no longer a question of nepotism.

The procedure at meetings of the Privy Council, of which I have only attended one, contains an anachronism from the past. Members of Council attending the Queen enter her presence in order of rank rather than of distinction. Had Sir Winston Churchill and I attended the same meeting, I would have preceded him.

Early in 1962 I had headed the British delegation to an economic conference of the Commonwealth held in New Delhi. An unlikely role, which evoked a caustic comment from Roy Jenkins when he read of it in a *Times* leader.

The President of India, Rajendra Prasad, gave a garden party for the delegates at his official residence, formerly Viceregal Lodge. The President, the humblest of men, contrasted strongly with all the pomp and panoply of his surroundings – his bodyguard was still on the same scale as that of the viceroys. The garden, too, was vast, formal in the immediate environs of the palace, then becoming similar to that of a large English country house. I explored it at leisure. Finding a gardener who spoke English, I asked how many gardeners there were. The answer was 'normally four hundred', but as the Queen had visited New Delhi that year an extra hundred had been taken on.

At the conclusion of the conference I was given a few days off. I did the usual tour of Agra and Jaipur. I saw the Taj Mahal under ideal conditions, at night, alone and under a full moon. It is so much reproduced in photographs that you know what you are going to see, it lacks the shock of the new. But the trick of the Taj Mahal is that, for all the received familiarity of its appearance, it still has a presence which leaves you silent and astonished.

I then went to Fatehpur Sikri, twenty miles away. I had no preconceived idea of the fortified palace built by Akbar but never finished; indeed I had never heard of it. My recollection is of walking up staircase after staircase and through huge rooms embellished with plaster. As you ascend the rooms become smaller and the decoration less rich, but even the unpretentious rooms at the top have traces of craftsmanship. In this it resembles Bess's Hardwick Hall. There, too, the great plaster frieze in the Presence Chamber is echoed by modest plaster decoration in the four rooftop rooms.

Akbar made a mistake in clearing the site for Fatehpur Sikri, since the water supply failed after thirteen years and it was abandoned incomplete. As with Pompeii and Siena, I found the atmosphere so strong that it gave you an eerie feeling of the presence of its creators.

After my time at the CRO I maintained a connection with the Commonwealth by becoming Chairman, and later President, of the Royal Commonwealth Society. As a result, in the late '60s, '70s and '80s I travelled widely over the Commonwealth, both the old Dominion countries and our former colonies. In spite of this continuing close connection with the Commonwealth I had doubts over its usefulness. It forms a club of former members of the Empire but many of these do not live up to the ideals of a modern democratic state.

Two memories of those travels. First, on a visit to the South Island of New Zealand the custodian of the albatross colony pulled off a masterpiece of tact. By giving no indication that he had previously shown me round, he spared me embarrassment with those who had arranged the visit. To be allowed to see these birds is an honour reserved for the privileged few, and I was dreading that the occasion might fall horribly flat.

Second, when I was visiting the botanical gardens in Halifax, Nova Scotia, I found at the entrance a group of weeping trees. Such planting is a trademark of Sir Joseph Paxton – there are several at Chatsworth. Commenting on the coincidence, I was told that Sir Joseph's grandson had been the first head gardener there.

The Kennedys

I was serving in Italy when the news came of my brother's engagement to Kathleen ('Kick') Kennedy. I was delighted but not surprised. We had known the family since 1938, when Joe Kennedy's children took the London Season by storm. My mother-in-law, Lady Redesdale, looked at Jack and remarked to Debo with impressive foresight that he might well become President of the United States. Kick, strictly speaking, wasn't beautiful but she had that Kennedy vitality. We liked her very much.

Joe Kennedy was American Ambassador in London. The biographical accounts of him grow harsher and harsher, but I shall restrict myself to saying that he hadn't the charm of his older children. The more distinguished members of the family took after their mother, Rose, the less distinguished after old Joe. He and my parents were an incongruous juxtaposition, thrown together now through the engagement of their respective offspring. The Kennedys' Roman Catholicism would have been a formidable problem: they were a very staunch Catholic family, while my mother and father, to put it mildly, would not have relished their son and heir marrying a Catholic if it meant that any children would have to be brought up in that faith. In the event Kick agreed that any son of the marriage should not be brought up as a Catholic, which caused much satisfaction to my family and was apparently accepted with good grace by the Kennedys. As it turned out, the marriage was childless. Billy was killed in action only four months after the wedding. Tragically, Kick herself was to lose her life in a flying accident in 1948. She is buried at Edensor, across the park from Chatsworth.

I still regard Rose Kennedy as one of the most remarkable people I have ever met. She was utterly unpretentious. On one occasion she came up to see Hardwick Hall. Having taken her over the house, there was some time to spare before her train left Chesterfield. For want of anything better to do, I took her round the town. As a former Parliamentary candidate for the constituency, I have a soft spot for Chesterfield but it's not among the Seven Wonders of the World. Perhaps it was just good manners, but Rose appeared intensely interested in everything I showed her. I told this story admiringly to a slightly acid-drop acquaintance and he suggested that being married to Joe she felt an affinity to the crooked spire.

She also had political antennae. One year in the early 1970s I toured the United States on a fund-raising mission for Israel. There was a meeting in Boston which she attended. For the first few minutes she applied herself to the purpose of the meeting, but then she was on to politics. Teddy was shortly due for re-election as the city's Senator.

The Kennedy family kept in touch with my family after Kick's death. In 1961 I had a brief diversion from my work with the Commonwealth Relations Office to attend Jack Kennedy's inauguration as President. Debo and I went to Washington, where we had been invited to the ceremony and the accompanying celebrations.

There was first a great ball given by a committee of leading Democrats, and the following morning the Inauguration in front of the Capitol. We were given privileged seats and, perhaps more important as it was so bitterly cold, I had a flask of whisky, supplied by a commendably practical secretary at our Embassy. The swearing in ceremony lasted about an hour and included a reading of his own poetry by Robert Frost. Afterwards we went by bus with the Kennedys to the White House. As we entered the gates they started to shout and sing 'We're coming, we're coming, hurray we're here, we're here and here we'll stay.' It was all rather engagingly schoolboyish, but infectious. A splendid luncheon followed, and afterwards came the march past at which the President took the salute. He, Bobby and Teddy were in tailcoats and top hats. American men are not accustomed to formal dress and so the brothers were amused by each other's appearance. I always remember the description of Hitler in morning dress looking like a cross between a chimney sweep and a head waiter. But whereas Hitler looked extremely uncomfortable about it, the Kennedys seemed to regard the whole thing as a good joke from the dressing up cupboard.

The parade was astonishing. There were the three armed services, many of whom wore galoshes and carried coats, interspersed with bands and drum majorettes. They constantly broke ranks to take photographs of the President standing on the dais. With my Brigade of Guards training, I felt like part of me wanted to put them all on a charge; but it wasn't just the lack of discipline – it seemed such a shame to lose the sense of ceremony. Whatever our shortcomings as a nation, that is something we are good at. You may dismiss it as theatre, but it's affecting theatre. A sense of ceremony runs through our public life. Judges love to process in wig and gown, and civic authorities from the Lord Mayor of London downwards can't wait to don their robes, tricorn hats and chains. Perhaps we are a nation of suppressed transvestites.

Debo and I went to Washington the following year for the opening of an exhibition of Old Master drawings from Chatsworth. This coincided with the Cuban missile crisis. We stayed with the Ambassador, David Harlech, my first cousin and close friend. David's position must have been unique in diplomatic history. Not only was he in the inner circle of the Kennedys' friends, but the President had great faith in David's judgement and frequently sought his advice. David's appointment to Washington was a stroke of genius by Uncle Harold. He had had it in mind prior to the Presidential Election of 1960. I remember he said to me when he was staying at Bolton Abbey in August of that year, that if Nixon won he would send a professional diplomat but that if Kennedy was successful the post would go to David, then Minister of State in the Foreign Office. Much has been written about the 'special relationship' between the United States and the United Kingdom. This was personified while Jack was President, Uncle Harold Prime Minister and David the Ambassador. David provided the vital link, the go-between. Friend and confidant of both, he became the instrument that forged the friendship between the two leaders. But for David I doubt whether the two men would have achieved such a degree of compatibility.

The Cuban crisis was inevitably the sole topic of conversation in Washington. We were due to fly back on the Sunday night. To my surprise a message was received saying the President wished to see David and me. At the last minute a second message came inviting Debo as well. David was surprised, since he had assumed the President had wished to see me as a member of our Government, perhaps, too, to give me a message for the Prime Minister. However, assuming now it was to be merely a social call, he rang the White House to ask if he should bring his wife, Sissie. No, came the reply, just the three of us.

It was late afternoon when we arrived. We had to push our way through a throng of officials and newspapermen to get into the Oval Office. In spite of the magnitude of the crisis, the President was completely relaxed. I learnt later that he had already taken his decision. We talked of the crisis for half an hour and then went for a walk in the garden. The President asked me how many gardeners there were at Chatsworth. I replied 'Twenty-one', to which he said 'Oh there are fifty here.' Miffed, I retorted 'Yes, Mr President, but I have to pay mine.' I will never forget his calmness and demeanour that afternoon when he must have been under intense strain. It was a sign of real calibre. Arriving in London on Monday morning the newspapers told me that the crisis was resolved.

My next visit to Washington, the following year, was to be in sad contrast.

I was in London on 22 November 1963. Returning to my house in Chesterfield Street at teatime I found Debo listening to the radio. She told me that Jack Kennedy had been shot. Such was his aura of immortality that we both supposed he couldn't have been seriously wounded. Within minutes we heard that he was dead.

I had to make an after dinner speech that night. I kept the engagement but whatever I was saying was of no consequence since all our minds were elsewhere.

In the ensuing years, like everyone else, I have pondered to what extent history was altered by the assassination. I have sought the views of those whom I respect on both sides of the Atlantic. Objective judgements are difficult to come by since Jack, with his style, charisma and arrogance, was a man whom people felt strongly about. You were for him or against him. He was not a man over whom you were neutral. But you tended to judge his presidency on whether or not you liked him.

The main question left unanswered by his death is, would the tragedy of Vietnam have been avoided had he lived? Of all those to whom I have put the question the man for whose judgement I have most respect was the late Sir Patrick Dean, our Ambassador in Washington from 1965 to 1969 and Permanent Representative of the UK to the United Nations from 1960 to 1964. He thought that American foreign policy making was too committed to a policy of intervention for Kennedy to change it even had he wished to. The episode of the Bay of Pigs casts doubts over what his inclinations would have been.

My mother felt that in view of the family connection Debo and I should attend his funeral. The Prime Minister concurred and we flew with him, the Duke of Edinburgh and the leader of the Opposition, Harold Wilson. On arrival in Washington we were met by David Harlech with the news that Lee Harvey Oswald, the man arrested for the assassination, had been shot dead. The funeral itself at Arlington Cemetery was highly emotional.

In 1968 came further terrible tragedy for the Kennedy family with the assassination of Bobby after winning the Californian primary in his campaign to stand as Democratic presidential candidate. Although he and I did not get on particularly well, my mother was anxious that I should go to the funeral to represent the family. Before I left, she said to me that although at funerals it was customary to keep in the background, she was anxious that the Kennedys should be aware that I had flown over for it. If there was a suitable moment, I should try to have some time with Rose.

I stayed the night in New York. The following morning saw the beginning of a most extraordinary day. Those attending the funeral in St Patrick's Cathedral had to be in place by 8 am. This meant by my standards an early start. I was not feeling at my best after the previous day's transatlantic flight. However, I managed to pull myself together and drove with my hostess, Mrs Ronnie Tree, to the cathedral. All the streets in central New York had been closed and the drive took only a few minutes. I found myself a place in the pews behind those to be occupied by the family.

The coffin was at the chancel steps and relays of distinguished men took it in turn to kneel at the four corners. The place was ringed with heavily armed policemen. It was full Mass and took an hour and a half. It must have been one of the strangest services in the history of the cathedral, because when it came to serving Mass to the hundreds of communicants, the priests were flanked by armed security guards.

The interment was to take place at Arlington Cemetery in Washington, so when the cathedral Mass was over we drove to Grand Central Station to catch the train. The roads were still closed to all other traffic. I found my way to a seat and was lucky enough to run into the American political journalist, Joe Alsop, a friend. In due course the train set off. At all vantage points there were crowds of people beside the railway line. I thought this would only be in New York, but it continued as we passed through the suburbs and even as we moved slowly into the countryside there were still people on both sides of the tracks, sometimes three or four deep, but always at least a single row. So it was all the way to Washington.

Eventually the train began to speed up and there followed a horrible accident. Some onlookers had spilled onto the track and four of them were mown down by the train. I was lucky enough not to see their mangled corpses, but many people did and it added a further bleak memory to an already sombre journey.

The organisers of the funeral had taken over Bobby's campaign train. It was very well equipped with bars and other facilities and packed with political heavyweights. After about an hour and a half members of the Kennedy family came down the train, shaking hands, explaining which member of the family they were – very much as if it were still a campaign occasion. When they all went back to the family coach, which was at the rear, I decided the moment had come for me to follow my mother's instructions.

As one entered the coach there was a bar, then came a drawing room which was occupied by members of the family and included David Harlech. Beyond this were two or three rest rooms. I learnt from the family that Rose Kennedy was free and they agreed to let me go in to see her.

Her composure was extraordinary. We talked of Bobby and Jack and of other members of the family. She did not mention the actual assassination, but rather talked around it. When I felt my time was up I made my farewells and found Mrs Martin Luther King waiting to make her courtesy call. I have often thought about that afternoon, and I believe her amazing resilience in the face of the family tragedies was entirely a matter of her religious faith. However shocking the events of this world that had overtaken her family, they were secondary to the expectations of the next.

After the accident the train again reduced speed and for the rest of the journey we moved very slowly. The result was that the journey from New York to Washington which should have taken four hours took slightly over eight – by which time it was dark. There were cars waiting to take us to the cemetery and troops lining the route from the station who must by now have been more than glad to see us pass. The service followed.

It was after the funeral that the organisation began to collapse. There were too few cars and by this time the air shuttle between Washington and New York had closed down. I had a bit of luck. Walking away from the terminal, I overheard a man say to another that he believed Governor Rockefeller had put his plane at the disposal of the press should they want to get back to New York. He also detailed where at Washington Airport it would be waiting.

Armed with this information I decided that what I required was a female companion. A middle-aged man on his own in a situation like this was not going to get very far. I was fortunate enough to see a very distinguished – though no longer young – lady sitting in one of the cars. I rather boldly opened the door, made what I hoped were reassuring noises, and said that I was very anxious to get back to New York that night. She said she was in exactly the same predicament – she had to catch a plane to Paris in the morning – and why didn't I get in. I then passed on the information I had heard about the Governor's plane and while I was doing so we were joined by three very charming American friends of the Kennedy family. They were only too glad to go out of their way to drop us back at the airport, and instructed the driver which way to go. Thanks to their kindness and the lady's charm – alas, I never discovered her name – we got to the airport and found the plane. I told the lady to say that she represented the *Daily Express* and I the *Daily Mail*. But we boarded the plane without being challenged.

The other two seats in my row were occupied by journalists who had been covering Bobby's campaign. They were talking about the service. One said to me 'You are English?' 'Yes.' He said 'Can you explain? At Jack's funeral there were twelve Heads of State, including General de Gaulle, your Duke of Edinburgh and so on, but tonight there was only our President.' Taken aback, but I hope hiding it, I said 'But Jack was President of the United States. Bobby, distinguished though he was, and quite possibly a future President himself, was only a Senator at the time of his death.' It was a perfect example of how the Kennedys were regarded as the Royal Family of the United States.

Racing

My family's connection with racing has been intermittent over the centuries. Our colours, 'straw', are the oldest registered on the Turf. The 1st Duke was a founder member of the Jockey Club. The 8th Duke won the 1,000 Guineas and the Ascot Gold Cup. In 1897 there was a great fancy dress ball at Devonshire House to mark Queen Victoria's Diamond Jubilee. To keep out of the way of the preparations the Duke spent the day at Newmarket.

My grandfather had some good horses, but sold them in the 1920s. The then Lord Rosebery, in a sorry misjudgement of my grandfather's character, put it about that he had only kept horses until he was elected a member of the Jockey Club. In fact my grandfather attached no importance whatever to being a member of the Jockey Club.

My father had no interest in racing. Luckily, his younger brother Charlie kept the straw colours going by owning horses in Ireland, and the Cavendish racing genes came into their own again with me and my son and younger daughter. Even at my preparatory school I would be cutting out racing photographs and sticking them in a scrapbook. I then had my precarious spell as school bookmaker at Eton. By the time I was at Cambridge I knew that racing would be a great love.

I bought my first flat racehorse in 1948. I sent it to Marcus Marsh at Newmarket, with whom I did not have much luck. Indeed I was generally considered by the racing fraternity as being an unlucky owner. Marcus had his share of success – he trained a couple of Derby winners in his career – but his enthusiasm for training declined and he retired in 1963.

After this I sent my horses to Bernard van Cutsem, who took over the Stanley House yard at Newmarket. Bernard, a friend of my brother Billy at Cambridge, had originally trained steeple-chasers and we all went racing together just before the war. After we were called up he and I had some contact in England before I was sent to Italy – he was in the Guards Armoured Division – and after the war we renewed our friendship. He bought Northmore House at Exning, outside Newmarket, where he built up a stud, and I used to stay with him for the Newmarket meetings. In 1957 he set up as a trainer. He was someone who inspired strong loyal-ties, but held strong opinions which didn't appeal to everybody. He was also a bit of a punter and that, when you're a trainer, can make the racing public suspicious of you – if only because it's so much in your interest to keep your inside information to yourself. But for me he was the closest and best of friends, the soul of generosity and integrity, with perfect manners; and a shrewd, hard-working and dedicated trainer. Our partnership turned out to be a great success. I have written of our association over my marvellous mare Park Top. Tragically, Bernard was struck down by cancer in 1969, but he would go down to Newmarket twice a week when the mare would do her major work. I like to think that training her with such success helped him through his suffering. The cancer recurred after a period of remission and he died in 1975.

If you care about racing, winning a race of any kind is a thrilling experience. Only one horse in six in training wins a race of any sort and countless thoroughbred foals never even make it on to the track. So it's a very expensive indulgence, full of frustrations and disappointments. That doesn't put you off; it merely makes the successes, when they come, all the sweeter. And sweeter they could hardly have been with Park Top. She didn't run as a two-year-old. As a three-year-old she won four races, including the Ribblesdale Stakes at Royal Ascot. As a four-year-old she won at Brighton and the Prix d'Hedouville at Longchamp. At five she won five times – twice at Longchamp, the Coronation Cup at Epsom, and the Hardwicke Stakes and the King George VI and Queen Elizabeth Stakes at Ascot – and was second in the Prix de l'Arc de Triomphe, the Eclipse Stakes at Sandown and the Champion Stakes at

Newmarket. For her achievements that season she was voted the Horse of the Year. The Arc is held on a Sunday and on the Monday afterwards I ran into a friend in London who said 'Sorry about yesterday, but you're pretty intolerable as it is. If you had won you'd have been quite intolerable.'

At six Park Top won La Coupe at Longchamp, the Cumberland Lodge Stakes at Ascot, and was second in the Coronation Cup at Epsom. If racing is lost on you, believe me, this is an owner's dream. Which is why her final defeat at Longchamp, ridden by Lester Piggott, was almost unbearably painful. I felt it was my fault and I had betrayed her. Let me quote from *Park Top*.

Understandably, the mare started a very hot favourite. Lester rode his usual race waiting at the back. We had no reason to feel unduly anxious as she turned into the straight with some ground to make up, for she was quite close enough to the leaders to win if she was good enough. Lester made his challenge a little earlier than on the other occasions he had ridden the mare. She made up some ground and for a few strides looked dangerous, but the brilliance had gone and for the first time in the nine races he had ridden her, she was unable to answer his call. I saw nothing of the closing stages of the race. Once I had seen she was not her true self and would not win I could not bear to watch. I was overwhelmed with self-reproach for allowing her to run after all she had done for me. In fact she dead-heated for third place with a filly called La Java. The race was won by Prime Abord by half a length from Hazy Idea.

... I have said of racing that the tears come when one wins and not when one loses. That October day in the Bois de Boulogne came near to being the exception. As we waited for her to return to be unsaddled I was close to tears, not tears of disappointment but tears of anguish for having let the defeat happen. Luckily, the unbelievable behaviour of the French crowd saved the day. As Park Top was led in, the Longchamp

Mayor and Mayoress of Buxton

'Lead, kindly Light': the mayoral procession in progress

Bolton Abbey, 1959: Hugh Fraser, the author, Harold Macmillan, Boofy Arran and Debo

Lagos, 1961: the Olori, the author, the Oba, Debo and Dot Head outside the Palace

Chatsworth, 1962: Evangeline Bruce (wife of the US Ambassador), Emma, Dorothy Macmillan, Debo, the President of India, the author, the President's wife, Toby Tennant

The Shah at Chatsworth, 1962: he stands between the author's mother and Debo, with (behind) the author's brother-in-law and sister, Michael and Anne Tree

ABOVE Sardauna of Sokoto comparing notes with Henry VIII at Chatsworth
BELOW The author in Borneo, 1964

The Kennedys visiting Kick's grave at Edensor ABOVE Bobby, Debo with Sophy, Ethel
Kennedy, January 1964 BELOW Joan and Teddy Kennedy with the author, May 1965

Peregrine Hartington's coming of age, 1965

Park Top wins the Prix Foy at Longchamp, 1969: Michael Ryan, Lester Piggott, the author, Debo and Bernard van Cutsem

Careysville House, Fermoy, Co. Cork and the River Blackwater

LEFT John O'Brien, the head ghillie tragically drowned at Careysville in 1964
RIGHT A sartorial warning, 1986: 'Never argue with a Cadogan'

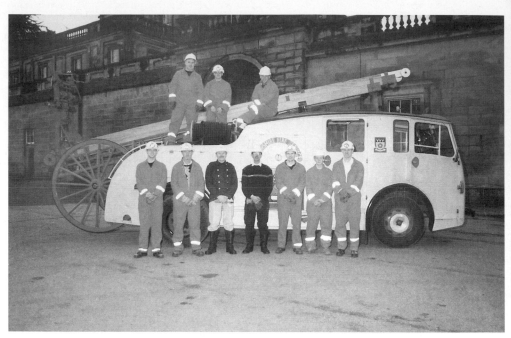

The Chatsworth Fire Team

The author and Sophy at the races

The Duchess of Devonshire, Pietro Annigoni. Devonshire Collection.

Portrait of an Old Man, Rembrandt, 1651. Devonshire Collection.

Tulips, from Thornton's *Temple of Flora*

Portrait of Girolamo Casio, Antonio Boltraffio. Devonshire Collection.

Head of a Woman (Lady Elizabeth Cavendish), Lucian Freud. Devonshire Collection.

Still Life, Nicolas Granger-Taylor. Devonshire Collection.

The Bellman, Samuel Palmer. Devonshire Collection.

Silver-gilt cup won by Park Top, King George VI and Queen Elizabeth Stakes

White Tulips, Wiliam Nicholson, 1912. Devonshire Collection.

race-goers began to boo. I could not believe my ears. For that crowd to boo Park Top, the mare they had taken to their hearts and from whom she had received as much, if not more, adulation than from race-goers in England, was like hearing a great prima donna being booed for faltering over one note. My anguish turned to fury ... [and I responded by showing them two fingers].

I will regret to my dying day that the mare was not retired after the Cumberland Lodge, but it had all looked so different before the race. I can still see the temptation of hoping to end her career with victories on the two courses in the two countries where she achieved such glory and received such acclaim. I have not been back to Longchamp and, unless I have a horse which my trainer insists on running there, I shall not go.

Having had the luck to own a mare like Park Top, I guessed that in most of my other forays into ownership on the Flat the law of averages would redress the balance and do its best to take the smile off my face. So, for the most part, it did. Compton Place, however, named after my family's house in Eastbourne, won the July Cup at Newmarket in 1997 and Teapot Row the Group II Royal Lodge Stakes at the Ascot Festival in September of the same year.

National Hunt racing is much more of a sport than flat racing. Stud value is rarely a key factor for the good reason that most of the horses running over fences and hurdles are geldings. I was exceptionally lucky with two horses, The Dunce and Gay George (named by an innocent Irish farmer), who won eighteen races between them. Peter Cazalet and Fulke Walwyn, both friends of mine, trained for me. Peter was not only a delightful man but a very clever one. He would have made a success of whatever career he chose, and certainly he was a successful trainer. Fulke was not clever but had a sixth sense in understanding horses. Very occasionally you come across people who have this extraordinary rapport with animals; and you can see the animals themselves respond to it. Fulke trained Gay George whose best success was winning the Scottish Champion Hurdle in 1982.

I would have liked to go on having jumpers but decided not to after both horses broke their necks in falls I witnessed. It was really too much for me. However, the old fire is not yet out and I still have half a dozen flat horses in training at Newmarket with James Toller. My younger daughter Sophy and granddaughter Celina love racing too, which is a joy; and I support their enthusiasms by giving them a horse each. I am glad to say they have both had a few successes.

Racing is a hard game. You have to be prepared to put up with plenty of disappointments. I have a number of friends, accustomed to being successful, who, I suspect, would like to become racehorse owners but are put off because they know that no matter how much money they put in, success is something they cannot be sure of.

You have your lucky and your unlucky courses. Although I won minor races at both, I considered York and Sandown unlucky – the latter with the abiding disappointment of Park Top's defeat in the 1969 Eclipse. She would have been the first filly to have won that race – a position in racing history she deserved. I liked and admired her jockey Geoff Lewis, but he got it wrong that day. He was the first to admit it and said to a mutual friend as he rode back into the unsaddling enclosure that he wished the ground would open up and swallow him.

Ascot has been a lucky course, led by Park Top's victories in the King George VI and Queen Elizabeth, the Ribblesdale, the Hardwicke and the Cumberland Lodge at the autumn meeting. Windsor too, although not a course of first importance, has also been outstandingly lucky for me: that was where Park Top won her first race, in a maiden in the spring of 1967. She was returned at the odds of 6-1; an astonishing price when you think of what she went on to do and the longest price she ever started at.

So far as prize money is concerned, this country is still the poor man of world racing, due to the fact that the bookmakers' profits take too much out of the industry. To visualise a Tote monopoly in this country is to cry for the moon and indeed racing without bookmakers would be, as I once remarked, like Trafalgar Square without the lions. In any event the clinching argument against the abolition of bookmakers would be that put forward by the Home Office – that it would inevitably lead to a vast escalation in illegal off-course betting.

When I became a Steward of the Jockey Club in 1967, times were changing. The 1961 Betting and Lotteries Act had brought about major changes in the administration of racing. For the first time taxpayers' money helped to support it. This was done by a levy, first on bookmakers' and the Tote's profits, and later amended to their turnover. The bookmaker passed this tax onto the punter. To run this side of racing a new body had been set up, known as the Horserace Levy Board, who had entire responsibility for the financial side. The Jockey Club remained the governing body for the running of racing, the planning of fixtures and the constant reviewing of the rules. It was my son who, on becoming Senior Steward of the Jockey Club in 1989, set about a major reorganisation. As a result the British Horseracing Board was created in 1993, taking over much of the work previously done by the Jockey Club. His tact ensured a minimum of friction between the Club, the old governing body, and the newly created BHB. The reforms were necessary; what was remarkable was that it had taken thirty years for it to become recognised that the Jockey Club was no longer a sufficiently accountable body to administer the sport. I regretted this, but I accepted it as inevitable.

It goes without saying that my son's part in all this gives me the utmost satisfaction. He was given the CBE in 1997 for his services to racing, and made the Queen's Representative at Ascot in 1998. He goes regularly to race meetings in the United States and is now a member of both the English and the American Jockey Clubs – a rarity.

Drink

ॐ

My good fortune has not been unmarred. Drink has run in the Cavendish family for generations. My father and his younger brother, Charlie, both suffered from what is generally acknowledged as the family weakness. Even the renowned 6th Duke (1790–1858) had his problems with it. The press remarked on occasions that when performing his duties as Lord Chamberlain he was observed as having unsteady hands due in all probability to an over-indulgence the night before. To most people the image of the plastered dignitary is comic, and what one might call social inebriation is generally thought a bit of a joke. But it would be hard to think of anything less amusing than dealing with drink as an addiction, both for the sufferer and the sufferer's family and friends.

The catch about alcohol of course is that it is selectively addictive. Most people can over-indulge without being in any way in its thrall; it has this dual personality as the good companion and the insidious destroyer. My own first meeting with what I choose to call the 'old enemy' was at Eton. A few friends used to meet in the backroom of the bootmakers in the High Street and drink white port during the long break between the end of morning school and boys' dinner. At Cambridge I and virtually all my friends drank a lot. While I was serving in England in the war Army discipline put a temporary check on my descent along the primrose path, but in Italy there was plenty of alcohol to hand – although one's responsibilities as an officer were obviously a restraining factor. Nevertheless, on the evening of my first night attack I drank a large quantity of orange juice mixed with NAAFI gin and issue rum. I don't think it made me brave but it stopped me feeling afraid.

When, with the end of the war, life resumed normality, it became clear that I was not to be excluded from the family malaise. As the years went by I became engaged in a losing battle. The signs of trouble were all there, but it was still over-indulgence rather than incapacitation; not sufficiently serious, for instance, to prevent me from joining the government in 1960, though the Prime Minister (even if not unsympathetic to those who enjoyed a drink) might well have thought twice before giving me a post. I did, to a very great extent, pull myself together during those four years, but no doubt there were occasional lapses.

I knew, increasingly, it was getting the better of me. The short-term bonhomie was merely a release from long-term depression. The drink didn't solve the problem, it merely staved off, for shorter and shorter spells, the effects of the depression it was actually making worse. I knew I was doing no favours to my family. I made periodic attempts to give up alcohol for varying lengths of time, from a few months to a time in the '70s when I gave up for two years, as the result of some drastic electric treatment.

By the early '80s I was an alcoholic. I would usually have my first drink at about midday (I get up very late!), wine with lunch and, as the problem got worse, an alarmingly early drink about 4 pm and a steady intake until I finally went to bed. I had vodka and ginger beer in the daytime and whisky in the evenings. This was very often private drinking. I was able, nevertheless, to lead an active life and meet any work commitments adequately, although I had nasty hangovers. What I particularly regret was that the drinking had a very bad effect on my manners. At home I was all too often rude to guests without any reason.

Things came to a final crisis in 1983. I managed to get off drink for a few weeks, then I went to a clinic in the West Country. There were nineteen of us, varying in age from teenagers to myself and one other in our sixties. It was the most dire experience of my life. Apart from the discomfort – sharing a room, one bathroom, two lavatories – I couldn't accept the whole ethic. Let me say at once that these were responsible, experienced people and their formula, as with the almost sub-religious commitment of Alcoholics Anonymous (with which I am also uncomfortable), must have had a measure of success. Not, however, with me. It consisted of conversations with a counsellor and group sessions with the other inmates. You had to bare your soul to diagnose the reasons for your problem. You had to take your mind to pieces and then rebuild it. This would help to exorcise the demon. You were asked to tell intimate details of your private life. My own – less tortuous – explanation, which was rejected, was that I simply liked the short-term effects of alcohol and hadn't the strength of will to give it up. Besides, to talk of my private life in front of strangers was out of the question. The course lasted six weeks. I stuck it for a fortnight. I was getting nowhere, so I left.

If I had stayed the full six weeks it would have destroyed me. Having no wish to see my family and friends I went to a hotel in Eastbourne. My hair – what there was of it – seemed to be even more shocked than I was. It stopped growing for three months. My spell in Eastbourne coincided with Wimbledon fortnight and I have never been able to watch the tournament on television since.

After this brief interlude I felt able to return to Chatsworth and slowly, but ever so slowly, resume a normal life. I started to drink again, though not to excess. Then one day the miracle occurred. I realised that apart from all the suffering I had caused, I was not my own master. I decided this slavery must stop once and for all. Easier said than done. I do not think that anyone who has been addicted to alcohol has the strength of character to give it up overnight. I persuaded my doctor to let me go into a nursing home for four days to get my bloodstream clear of alcohol. I was then free to take 'Antabuse'. One pill each morning ensures that should one drink anything one feels extremely ill.

While in the past I used to ensure that alcohol was always readily available, now an ample supply of Antabuse tablets was top of the list. The early months – and indeed years – were often difficult. There were occasions when I would have given anything for a drink although I already realised how much simpler life was now without the hangover and the remorse. Thanks to the support of my family, and perhaps assistance from Above, I held on. Twenty years later I am still a teetotaller. Social life is infinitely more limited. I used to be very gregarious, a great club man. Now I prefer the company of my family and a few close friends. But of all the challenges in my life I put the defeat of the old enemy at the very top.

Looking back on my time as an alcoholic I can only be horrified. I seemed oblivious to the suffering I was causing and that remains something I have to live with. It is, of course, a common failing, some would say an illness. But, given the will, it can be overcome. In my case it has left an indelible stain on my life. To anyone reading these pages and suffering a similar problem I can tell them that alcoholism can only be defeated by determination.

Ireland

ʒᴗ

L ismore Castle, in Co. Waterford in the Republic of Ireland, stands on a crag with the Blackwater flowing eighty feet below. It came into Cavendish ownership through female inheritance in the middle of the eighteenth century. The view from the castle is spectacular – west and east up and down the river, with wooded hills on the far bank to the north and the Knockmealdown Mountains six miles away as a backdrop. The main road from the north crosses the Blackwater over a seven-arch bridge and then climbs steeply to the town with the cathedral of St Carthage on the left and the castle on the right.

It was built in 1185, before his accession, by King John on the site of the old Lios (fort) near the 'double monastery' founded by St Carthage. In 1589 it was leased – and later bought – from the Bishop of Lismore by Sir Walter Raleigh. Raleigh, whose only long-term legacy to Ireland was reputedly the planting of its first potatoes, had been awarded three and a half seignories by the Crown, 42,000 acres, in Cork, Munster and Waterford. However, as a largely absentee landlord and presumably stretched by his wider role as 'fortune's tennis ball', as one of his contemporaries described him, he found the administrative and financial pressures too much and in 1602 he sold the seignories to the 1st Lord Boyle, later Earl of Cork – the 'Great Earl'. It was the Boyle connection that was to be of such importance to my family.

The Great Earl was buried in 1643 in St Mary's Collegiate church in Youghal (the resting place, too, of the Countess of Desmond, who died in 1604 at the reported age of 140 after falling out of an apple tree – a very odd venue for one's twilight years). The Irish title and the extensive possessions both in Ireland and England passed to the Great Earl's son, created 1st Earl of Burlington in the

English peerage in 1664. It was he who acquired and completed Burlington House on the north side of Piccadilly, now home of the Royal Academy.

His grandson, the 3rd Earl, a major patron of the arts and friend of Alexander Pope, had two daughters but no surviving son. One daughter married the Earl of Euston, the heir to the 2nd Duke of Grafton; the other married Lord Hartington, heir to the 3rd Duke of Devonshire. The Euston marriage produced no children, both parties dying comparatively young, so Lady Hartington inherited everything. This brought new estates to the family including Londesborough Hall and Bolton Abbey in Yorkshire, Burlington House and Chiswick House in London and, of course, Lismore Castle, plus all Lord Burlington's architectural books and drawings, many important paintings which became the nucleus of the Cavendish collection and the contents of all the houses.

At the time Lismore became Cavendish property the castle was a ruin, having been burnt down during the time of the rebellion against Cromwell. It remained a ruin until the first part of the nineteenth century, when the 6th Duke ('the Bachelor Duke') applied himself to rebuilding it. William Atkinson was the principal architect of the restoration work of 1812–22, with the dressed stone brought from Derbyshire. Two reminders were uncovered of Lismore's holy origins – the Lismore Crosier, inscribed to Nial MacAeducain, Bishop of Lismore, who died in 1113, and the Book of McCarthy Reagh, popularly known as the Book of Lismore, containing important accounts of the lives of some early Irish saints.

The interiors were largely the creation of Crace and Pugin after 1850. The Bachelor Duke's henchman Joseph Paxton, later Sir Joseph of Crystal Palace fame, added to the south and east wings. There are some of the Elizabethan buildings still extant, but most of what one sees today is nineteenth century. While many of the rooms are small, there is a magnificent drawing room and – Pugin's triumph – a spectacular Banqueting Hall. Currently the estate runs to 10,859 acres, with a further 618 acres of forestry let to the

Minister for Lands on a 150-year lease at a peppercorn rent. There is a magic about Lismore, it looks the perfect fairy-tale castle. Debo and I have spent some of the happiest times of our lives there.

In justice, I should not have inherited it. My grandfather gave Lismore to my father's younger brother, Charlie, as a wedding present, together with farmland, woods and excellent fishing. The property had been considerably reduced in 1921 on Ireland's independence, but it was still substantial. Charlie married Adele Astaire, Fred's elder sister and erstwhile dancing partner. They had no children, so Charlie left Lismore to his widow for her life unless she remarried, in which case it was to come to me as the younger son. Had he not died while my brother Billy was still alive, it would surely have been left to another member of my family.

In the event Charlie died a few months before Billy was killed. In July 1946, at her invitation, I went to see Adele at Lismore. She told me she wished to remarry provided satisfactory financial arrangements could be made. Thanks to my father's generosity this became possible and in the spring of the following year Debo and I went there as owners for the first time.

While not beautiful, Adele had tremendous vitality; and in this regard, even if their language was very different (Adele was what one might call broad of expression), she had something in common with my sister-in-law Kick – though I am not sure that Kick would have been gratified by the comparison. Fred, a regular at Lismore, was delightful and we shared a strong common interest in horse racing. Indeed when my mare Park Top won the King George and Queen Elizabeth Stakes at Ascot, Fred's was almost the first message of congratulation. I remember we went to see him backstage during the London stage production of *The Gay Divorce* – I was still a schoolboy – and he was delighted to find I had a racing form book in my pocket. The musical, when turned into a film, was retitled *The Gay Divorcee* on the insistence of the Hayes Office in Hollywood on the grounds that divorce should not be regarded as something light-hearted.

I had been introduced to salmon fishing by my father and it

became one of my lifelong passions. Many of the most contented hours of my life have been spent on the banks of the Blackwater. I don't think I was ever more conscious of tranquillity and natural harmony; and yet I have sometimes found myself unsettled about the relationship between the hunter and the hunted. It doesn't fluster Nature, but we are uneasy about confronting our own primitive instincts. I tried to persuade myself that the edibility of salmon was a factor in the argument. It isn't of course, any more than the itchy refutation that begins 'It's no worse than ...' answers charges of cruelty that are themselves too often over-simplified. I don't shoot, but I watch others; and my views are on record about the abolition of hunting. These are emotive issues; but I should have thought that people with first-hand experience of them would be more likely to arrive at reasonable conclusions.

Soon after the war we bought the fishing at Careysville, sixteen miles upstream, the best beat on the Blackwater. For the salmon fisher it was near-perfection, though it was to suffer later from both the offshore netting and the onset of salmon disease. In the last decade, when all the salmon rivers have faced hard times, the spring run has seriously deteriorated but the summer run of grilse has held up well. And the setting is hard to match.

Nevertheless, for me the halcyon years at Careysville came to a poignant end in 1964. I had been over to Lismore in that September to convalesce after an illness. The garden was lovely, the fishing excellent. I returned to London renewed. Then, on the evening of 17 November, I was at the House of Lords when a telephone message came through to say that three ghillies employed at Careysville had drowned. I left for Lismore at once, to discover that the ghillies, in the course of their duties in mending the banks, had endeavoured to cross the river when it was running too high for safety. One of them had panicked and stood up, thus overturning the boat. All three men had been my companions. One, Johnny O'Brien, my own particular ghillie, I had come to regard as a guide, philosopher and friend. I eventually returned to fish at Careysville, but it was never the same. The year after the accident I had a stone

Celtic cross put up to commemorate the tragedy. Flowers are placed at its foot on 17 November every year.

The other great attraction of Lismore, as far as I am concerned, is the gardening. Gardening in Derbyshire is difficult unless you go for the hardiest of plants and shrubs. But at Lismore you can grow tender species, perhaps not quite so well as in Devon and Cornwall as there is less sunshine, but the horticultural climate is similar. Magnolias, rhododendrons and camellias all flourish and over the years the garden has been an ever-increasing pleasure. It is divided into two parts by the drive. The western half, bound by a wall dating back to King John, is chalk and is in a series of terraces containing herbaceous borders and an orchard with a modest greenhouse. At some time in the nineteenth century vast quantities of peat were dug into a number of beds in the eastern half. It was an amazing achievement and as a result that eastern half contains a fine collection of rhododendrons and magnolias, including *Magnolia sprengeri diva* and the finest of all, *campbellii*. In these latter years my son has added enormously to the attraction of the garden with the introduction of modern sculpture, including work by Anthony Gormley (of Angel of the North fame) and Eilis O'Connell. The garden is open to the public, but as the house is frequently let (usually to Americans) it is not possible for that to be opened. But it is a source of continuing pleasure to me that my son and his family love the place, the garden and the decoration both thrive, and last year (2003) my granddaughter Jasmine chose to be married there. So the family connection with Lismore is as strong as ever.

Even after living there for part of each year for the past fifty years, and counting many Irishmen as my friends, I don't feel included in their Irishness. The truth is that any Englishman, even one whose family have owned property in Ireland over the centuries, is still regarded as English. A stay at the castle by Edward VII, of which there are photographs in one of the bedrooms, was belatedly counterpointed by Mary Robinson, who honoured us with a visit as President of the Republic and planted a tree. It is impossible to take part in any form of public life, other than perhaps with the Red Cross or the Royal British Legion. The question of religion, admittedly, is less of an issue in the South than it is in Ulster. Membership of the Protestant Church of Ireland is no barrier to being regarded by the Roman Catholic community as a true Irishman. But for me the Republic is a mistress rather than a wife, to be visited but not to live with. Around Lismore you are greeted with relaxed perfect manners wherever you go; I find I don't worry; and I find I can't work. Years ago when I was in government I used to take a box of papers whenever I went over for a long weekend. On my return the contents had never been touched.

What was irksome, though hardly a criticism of the Irish authorities, was that after I became a Minister and up until 1995 there was always a strong Garda presence when my family were staying at Lismore. It meant you had armed protection even when you were going round the garden and certainly when you were fishing.

I used to be a very keen walker and I liked the challenge of climbing the Knockmealdown Mountains. One day I walked from the castle to the foot of the climb, just over six miles. I was followed by a police car all the way, and when I took to the hill the car remained on the road. I duly made it to the top and down again, and then walked home – the police car following. The policeman never left the car, yet the next morning he said to Debo, 'Dear God, we had a terrible trek yesterday.'

Books and Collecting

❧

My father, grandfather and even the 8th Duke were not collectors. They thought, with justification, that the Devonshire Collection of works of art, accumulated largely by the 2nd, 4th and 6th Dukes through astute purchases or equally astute marriages, and one of the finest private collections, was sufficient. They freewheeled. As with horse racing, I have reverted to earlier generations.

First, books. My sitting room, with shelves all around filled with books I have collected, is where I spend by far the greatest part of my time – especially now I am infirm. I have two shelves reserved for friends who are authors: Paddy Leigh Fermor is the most distinguished (and an admirable mentor in the selection of reference books), but there others of no particular literary distinction whose friendship gives their authorship a special attraction: Daphne Bath (later Fielding), for instance, and Michael Astor, Nancy Astor's third son, whose *Tribal Feeling* is an excellent study in family relations. (My mother and her distinguished literary brother, David Cecil, were much taken by a sentiment from Jane Austen – 'Family life is all very well for those who can stand it'. This was written in capital letters and stuck into the edge of a looking glass in the drawing room at Churchdale in my youth.)

I think my bibliophile tendency came from David Cecil, although, perversely, I was initially put off being read to – and that has extended to talking books – because David and my mother overdid it. (My father's over-indulgence was in taking me to the zoo too often: and that scotched my enthusiasm for zoos.) But both my parents were keen readers. My father, a fluent French speaker, was fond of French novels and it was the trouble my mother took over the bedroom books at Churchdale that led me to follow her example at Chatsworth. Restocking the guest bedrooms is an annual Christmas task I much enjoy. The fact that only a tiny minority of those coming to stay here read the books or even look at them does not deter me from trying to provide a miniature library in each room that should satisfy a wide range of taste. If author friends come to stay I ensure they will find in their room at least one of their own books discreetly included.

The basic ingredients are *The Oxford Book of English Verse*, *The Oxford Book of Short Stories*, *The Oxford Book of English Prose* (and latterly *The New Oxford Book of English Prose*, edited by John Gross, an ex-judge on our Heywood Hill Literary Prize), a volume each of Henry James's and Saki's short stories, and P. G. Wodehouse. I then build on that platform.

The Chatsworth library is famous. Guests gaze at it in rapt admiration, but I cannot remember a single one, since we returned here in 1959, asking to take a book out to read. My own interest has been to add a collection of twentieth-century titles as well as a collection of illustrated flower books. It is surprising, given the 6th Duke's devotion to gardening and his close association with Joseph Paxton, that flower books were not better represented in the library I inherited. Perhaps the best-known titles I have added are Redouté's *Les Roses* and *Les Liliacées*, his collection of lilies in 500 plates, and Thornton's *Temple of Flora*. Others include the ten volumes of J. Sibthorp, *Flora Graeca* (1840); William Jackson Hooker and Walter Fitch, *Description of the Victoria Regia, or Illustrations of the Royal Water-lily of South America* (1851); John Fisk Allen, *Victoria Regia; or the Great Water-lily of America* (1854); and Georg Dionysius Ehret, *Plantae et Papiliones Rariores Depictae*, issued as a series of plates from 1748 and collected in 1759 as this volume.

The fiction shelves are manned by all the stalwarts, from Dickens, Trollope and Hardy up through the twentieth century. There is the delightful pocket edition of Henry James and two editions of Proust to reproach me for having never got beyond the second volume – the lesser-known translation by Stephen Hudson (1949)

illustrated by Philippe Jullian, of which I have a number of the orig-
inals, and the 1982 version translated by Scott Moncrieff and
Kilmartin. One of the highlights of the non-fiction collection is a set
of first editions of Sir Winston Churchill's works, including the
much-prized red paper-covered pamphlet on India. Bloomsbury is
well represented, including, obviously, Leonard Woolf's autobiog-
raphy, a favourite of mine. I also have a complete set of *Horizon*.

There are nice quirks, too. One is a shelf devoted to disasters, an
idea I copied from Paul Mellon (the greatest gentleman I ever met),
who had a similar shelf in his library. The biography of the Duke of
Windsor spends alternate years with disasters, but is otherwise
promoted to the shelves containing biographies of all the nation's
monarchs and prime ministers.

I have tried to cover the war years. Sir John Wheeler-Bennett's
The Nemesis of Power: The German Army in Politics 1918–1945
is masterly. I have a sentimental attachment to Nigel Balchin's
compelling *A Small Back Room*, which I was reading the night
before I first went into action in Italy – so much so that I gave no
thought to what the following day might hold; and in July every
year I return to Lyn Macdonald's *Somme*, to remind me of the
unspeakable horrors of the First World War. It conjures up the visits
I used to make to the Continental platforms at Victoria, when I
would imagine those eight-carriage trains, seven loaded up with
soldiers going to the Western Front and, for many of them, an average expectation of death within a fortnight, while in the eighth the
hated staff with their red lapels were giving orders for drinks in the
reassurance of security behind the line.

My swan-song is the building up of a comprehensive library on
all aspects of life in the history of Ireland. I decided on this because
of my family's connection, centred on Lismore; and also because
Home Rule (to which he was opposed) played an important part in
the 8th Duke's political career.

What is painfully inappropriate for a bibliophile is that I now
suffer from a relatively rare disease of the eyes known as senile
macular dystrophy. I understand this means the cells in the pupils

are dead. The result is that, while I can see, my eyesight is badly impaired. I can only read through strong magnifying glasses, which makes the reading of books virtually impossible because of the length of the lines.

The London bookshop Heywood Hill in Curzon Street, only round the corner from my house in Chesterfield Street, had always been a favourite port of call. Nancy Mitford, my sister-in-law, worked there during the war and indeed there is now a blue plaque in her honour on the outside of the building. I heard that a controlling interest in the shop was for sale, so in September 1991, with the approval of my financial advisers, I bought it. John Saumarez Smith, who still runs the shop (and I can't imagine him having an equal as a bookseller), had long been a friend and helped me in building up the library in my sitting room.

Four years later I decided that the shop should give an annual literary prize – the Heywood Hill Literary Prize – awarded for a lifetime's contribution to the enjoyment of books. (The Man Booker and the Whitbread, by contrast, are awarded for individual works.) Since its inception the winners have included Patrick O'Brian, Penelope Fitzgerald, Jane Gardam, Charles Causley, Michael Holroyd and Michael Frayn, and those presenting the prize have included Tom Stoppard, P. D. James, John le Carré and J. K. Rowling. John Saumarez Smith is chairman of the judges, the other two judges each serve for two years. One of the first two judges was Roy Jenkins, the most recent Ferdinand Mount, himself an admired author and until fairly recently a long-term editor of the *Times Literary Supplement*. I attend the meetings and hold the right of veto, though I have never had to use it. We meet in January to decide on a short list and, after the judges have had time to do a good deal of reading, meet again in May to agree on the winner. I suspect it is regarded in some quarters as a faintly ridiculous ducal indulgence. Up to now the press in the main have treated it with determined indifference. That sort of silent statement is uncomfortably easy to hear.

The prizegiving is held in early June at Chatsworth and those attending it have been described as the 'literati and glitterati' – the latter referring to the Derbyshire mayors and chairmen of council, who turn out in force in their chains of office. Two bands play during the afternoon and there is, I hope, a liberal supply of Pimm's spiked with gin. There is always a wonderful turnout (a number of friends from America come specially for the occasion) and an atmosphere of good humour, which is heartening – especially as, for many of the people present, Chatsworth is not next door.

The works of art that had to be sold for death duties are irreplaceable, but over the years I have also collected pictures, sculpture and, following the tradition of Georgiana Duchess and her son, the 6th Duke, minerals – several large specimens like a giant amethyst crystal in the West Hall which Debo gave me for Christmas 2002, and a section of fossil tree trunk, and the locally-mined stones which are now almost worked out – Blue John (veined fluorspar) and Duke's Red Marble (actually alabaster). The 6th Duke commissioned the largest Blue John vase ever made from a single piece, c. 1842, which is in the Sculpture Gallery. There are also many pieces from all over the world in the form of geodes, fossils, corals and crystals. They include specimens of the same vivid green malachite one sees in the Russian malachite table and clock the 6th Duke received as a gift from Czar Nicholas I (in the State Music Room at Chatsworth).

An early stroke of luck was when, in Bond Street in 1946, I ran into a fellow officer from Italy, Peter Tunnard. He said even I would have heard of Augustus John, but did I know the work of his sister Gwen, who was then having a show? He thought Gwen was the better artist. Having seen for myself, I agreed with him. I bought three of her pictures – two portraits and a view of her studio which I gave to my sister Anne as a wedding present.

It was through Anne that I became a friend of Lucian Freud. I commissioned him, before he became so famous, to paint Debo, my two sisters, my mother and myself, and he gave me a sketch of our son. I also have a number of his drawings and a very early (1936) linocut of a galloping horse, and in 1974 I persuaded my Trustees to buy one of his major works, *Large Interior W9*. Debo has a painting of a baby on a sofa and a self-portrait of Lucian in a hospital bed and has recently acquired another painting, *Four Eggs on a Plate*.

Other acquisitions have been an unusual riverscape of Maryport by Lowry; *White Tulips* by William Nicholson, a picture I particularly like; works by Sickert, Augustus John and Elizabeth Blackadder; and a lovely portrait of the pre-war actress Gladys Cooper by Ambrose McEvoy, which I bought from her son-in-law, Robert Morley. I have also collected a number of paintings by Adolphe Valette, Lowry's mentor, a considerable artist in his own right but not fashionable. My most recent acquisitions have been one anonymous portrait and a number of still lives by Nicolas Granger-Taylor. I have a very high regard for his work. Other additions have been still lives by David Denby, and *Madonna No. 1 (Victorian Mood)* by an unknown Chesterfield artist called Gordon Liddle, who deserves to make a name for himself. In London I have two works by Paul Wunderlich, *La Femme entre les Deux Ages* (1991) and *Du Solt Nit Umkeusch Sien* (1990) – not everyone's taste; Andrew Hemingway's *Still Life with Red Apple on Marble Blocks* (1999); Hector McDonnell's *Kennedy's Sausage Shop off Walworth Road* (1973); and a study of a birch tree trunk by Duncan Wood, a local artist from Baslow who was recommended to me by Lucian Freud.

In 1976, at my instigation, my Trustees bought two watercolours by Samuel Palmer illustrating Milton's 'Il Penseroso', *Morning* and *The Bellman*. The purchases were made at the time of Tom Keating's exposure as a prolific forger, with Samuel Palmer prominently in his repertoire. I took great care to check that my pictures were authentic and they have since been verified, but in view of the publicity they were probably cheaper than they would have been otherwise.

A chance meeting in November 1964 with the sculptress Angela

Conner began a long and fruitful association. I went to her studio the following day where there was a recently completed head of Roy Strong, which I bought and at the same commissioned her to do one of Uncle Harold. Since then she has done heads of my family and friends, most of them on display in the Sculpture Gallery at Chatsworth – my son, my elder daughter Emma, my grandson William, myself, the Prince of Wales, John Betjeman, Paddy Leigh Fermor, Lucian Freud, Tom Stoppard. In London her most visible work is the eleven-foot statue of de Gaulle on a plinth in Carlton Gardens. (Somewhat inappropriately, the similar version in Paris is only three foot six.)

Angela is extremely adept at posthumous heads – one of my much-lamented trainer Bernard van Cutsem, another of a prominent figure on the Turf, the late Lord Wigg, and, for Eton, Alec Douglas Home. The College also has a head of Uncle Harold. Angela's own preferences are for the heads of Lucian, my daughter Emma and Noël Coward. Of the latter there is one in the Theatre Royal, Drury Lane, one in his former home in Jamaica and one in the Hall of Fame at the Gershwin Theatre in New York. In 2003 I commissioned her to do two posthumous heads of the Queen Mother, which were unveiled by the Queen at her mother's favourite racecourses, Sandown and Cheltenham. I am hopeful that Angela may be permitted soon to do a head of the Queen to be placed in an appropriate situation in St George's Chapel, Windsor.

While portrait heads are Angela's bread and butter, her real love is water sculpture. In 1999 she created an astonishing, imaginative fountain for the garden at Chatsworth, which, over a period of five minutes, opens and closes. I named it *Revelation*. She has also made the tallest sculpture in Europe for Park West in Dublin, and her work *Poise* was commissioned for Chesterfield town centre.

I have bought a number of bronzes from a young sculptor called Tom Freeston, who lives in France but whose parents live near Chatsworth. Some are wild life subjects, some more abstract pieces. My most recent acquisition, which will be placed in the Sculpture

Gallery, is his bronze of Brunel's hat, which I have had put onto a high pillar.

If I had to choose six favourites from what I inherited and six favourites from what I have acquired, the list would be: in the first category, Canova's head of Napoleon; Rembrandt's *Portrait of an Old Man*; Nicolas Poussin's *Et in Arcadia Ego*; Giovanni Antonio Boltraffio's portrait of Girolamo Casio with a skull on the reverse, c. 1500, once attributed to Leonardo da Vinci; (as one item) the two Franz Hals portraits; Rubens's drawing *Peasant Girl Churning Butter*. In the second category: Lucian Freud's *Large Interior W9*; Angela Conner's head of Lucian, which is placed by his picture; William Nicholson's *White Tulips*; Lowry's riverscape of Maryport; the silver-gilt cup for winning the King George VI and Queen Elizabeth Stakes with Park Top (to remind me of my finest hour in racing); Thornton's *Temple of Flora*. An added satisfaction about the Nicholson and the Lowry is that they were bought with Park Top's winnings.

Chatsworth

Debo and I divide the administration of Chatsworth between us: which, put another way, means she does practically everything and my responsibilities – appropriately for a partially sighted tee-totaller – are books and wine. But I did play a key role in helping to secure the whole enterprise in setting up the Chatsworth House Trust in 1980.

The opening of Chatsworth to the public had proved a great success. In the early years numbers visiting the house grew steadily. The charges for admittance were reviewed each year and gradually increased. Nevertheless, in spite of this vital support from the visiting public, it was soon clear that their contribution would not pay for the upkeep of the house. The shortfall had to be met from revenue from the estate. For some time I had realised that the maintenance of such a vast house was too heavy a burden for an agricultural estate.

To have to rely on present-day agricultural rents, even if they are sporadically supplemented by sales of outlying parts of the estate, is a difficult task. I decided that it was not fair on Derrick Penrose, who had succeeded Hugo Read as agent, to ask him to provide finance to meet the shortfall in the running costs.

Once again the wisdom and advice of my financial and legal advisers, Messrs Currey and Co, was vital. It was decided that a major change should take place. The ownership of the house, garden and park would become the property of a charitable trust. A precedent for this kind of ownership had been established at Leeds Castle. I sought the advice of the Leeds Trustees, who were extremely helpful.

A charitable trust of this nature appealed to me infinitely more than handing the house over to the National Trust. I have the utmost admiration for the work done by the Trust – indeed my daughter Emma was chairman of its Garden Panel; and their administration of Hardwick Hall is beyond praise. All the same I could never accept the idea of living at Chatsworth as their tenant. I couldn't bear to have to seek permission to redecorate a room or put in a new bathroom. I have no doubt that the National Trust would have accepted Chatsworth as one of its properties, but it would rightly have asked an enormous endowment.

A substantial sum of money was required to set up the House Trust. This was, in the main, provided by the sale of Poussin's *Holy Family*. To sell such a picture was painful, but a price well worth paying. Books were also sold, so that a capital sum was established to provide an income which, together with the revenue from visitors, meets the cost of the upkeep of Chatsworth and its immediate surroundings. In 2003 there were approximately 472,000 visitors to the house and garden.

In all probability this capital sum will have to be supplemented to meet the ever-increasing maintenance costs. This may mean the sale of further works of art, or I may be able to provide money from personal sources. So far Chatsworth has never received any direct financial assistance from the state. I am determined this independence will continue for my lifetime. I feel strongly on this point for two reasons – I regard it as unbecoming, to put it mildly, that when I am blessed with so much material good fortune I should call on taxpayers' money to enable me to live in the style I do. Second, provided there is no state assistance I am in no way beholden to any government as to how Chatsworth is administered.

The setting up of the Chatsworth House Trust meant ceding family authority over Chatsworth, in that the independent directors must be in a majority over family representatives. However, we have been lucky in finding men and women of distinction willing to serve in this capacity. Our principal bi-annual meetings are happy occasions and I like to think that these directors have come to regard themselves as members of the family.

As to the future, so long as my family lives in the house the

Chatsworth House Trust will be a blessing. Should the day come when, for economic reasons or by personal reasons of choice, my son or my grandson wishes to live elsewhere, then it will be a different matter. The money in the House Trust can never be taken out, its purpose being the maintenance of Chatsworth. While I hope and believe my son may bless me for setting up the Trust, it may well be that my grandson and his successors may regret such large sums of money being set aside to maintain a property in which they find themselves unable to live. I worry about that, but it is impossible to see more than a certain number of years ahead and I hope the establishment of the House Trust will enable Chatsworth to continue to enjoy what I sincerely believe to be the real benefit of being a family home at least well into this century.

The logistics are formidable. The house, with more than 300 rooms, is huge, the garden is 100 acres, the park 1,100. Beneath Chatsworth's 1.3 acres of lead roof there are 3,426 feet of passages, 17 staircases, 3 lifts and 359 doors, all lit by 2,084 light bulbs (you must guess at the total wattage). There are 397 external window frames, 62 internal window frames, 5 roof lanterns and 60 roof lights, with a grand total of 7,873 panes of glass. To complete the barrage of statistics throw in 30 baths, 59 hand basins, 29 sinks, 6 wash-ups and 64 lavatories.

Currently, total expenditure of the Chatsworth House Trust is approximately £4 million per annum. This includes up to £½ million spent annually on special jobs (over and above annual running costs), such as renewal and restoration of the fabric of the house and stables; stonework, garden buildings and waterworks, cleaning of painted ceilings and walls, major furniture conservation and even bug control.

Belonging to the Chatsworth Settlement Trustees, the estate takes in the villages of Edensor, Pilsley and Calton Lees, and estate workers also live in parts of Beeley and Baslow. The main estate comprises 4,982 hectares (12,310 acres) surrounding the house; the west estate comprises 2,630 hectares (6,498 acres) including land

and houses at Bakewell, Ashford, Wetton, Monyash and Buxton (most of this high ground is made up of stock-rearing farms). The Shottle estate comprises 1,424 hectares (3,518 acres) of farms and buildings in and around Shottle, near Belper (this land is suited to stock and arable enterprises and the majority of Chatsworth's dairy farmers live here). The Staveley estate, north east of Chesterfield, comprises 1,376 hectares (3,400 acres) of both farmland and industrial sites, and the Scarcliffe estate, east of Chesterfield, comprises 3,772 hectares (9,320 acres) of mostly arable farms, woods and houses in and around Elmton, Whaley, Scarcliffe, Heath, Rowthorne and Palterton (the M1 was constructed through part of this land in 1968 and the land at Junction 29 was purchased from Chatsworth).

The workforce, under the direction of the agent and deputy agent, the comptroller, the clerk of works and the keeper of collections, is about 286 full time and 226 part time employees. (This compares interestingly with 1955 when the full and part time jobs totalled 180.) They include electricians, plumbers, painters, a mason, seamstresses, housekeepers, gardeners, domain men, farmers, foresters, gamekeepers, security men, telephonists, drivers and other general maintenance staff. A further small army help to look after our visitors – in the shops, restaurant, farmyard and adventure playground and the education service. The estate community immediately surrounding the house, including pensioners and children, is approximately 450. We are extremely fortunate in the skills, loyalty and dedication of all the staff here. It is my responsibility to ensure that they are properly looked after, and if that invites the charge that the whole setup is paternalistic, I can only agree; but I do not see how it could be run in any other way.

Housing is one of the main problems with which I am faced. About 170 houses on the estate are lived in by staff and pensioners. The old estate office has been turned into flats for the widows and widowers of estate pensioners and recently we built two bungalows for pensioners in Pilsley. When places do become available the rival claims are often difficult to assess. There is either a pressing need to find new houses for those married with growing families, or suddenly there are empty ones which we do not want to let to people outside the estate, knowing full well that they will be required in the near future. It is a constant problem. But happily most employees want to live on the estate and are patient in waiting for the house of their choice.

There has always been a cricket club and a bowling green, but the estate golf course had been incorporated into the farm. So some years ago I reconstituted the course on a nine-hole basis with eighteen tees. I wouldn't pretend it's championship standard, but it is immensely popular and golf has become the main outdoor social activity. We have started up golf lessons for the children at Pilsley School, we have both men's and ladies' cricket teams who have played against my grandson's XI and now a ladies' football team is about to begin training. There is also a swimming pool, a tennis court and, most recently, a gymnasium where members use its treadmill machines in manic fashion in spite of the fact that Chatsworth is within a few miles of the Peak District and some of the best walking country in the kingdom. It is an odd example of energetic indolence.

Again, though it may sound too feudal for some readers, the continuity of some of the Chatsworth families is a sign of our good fortune. The Olivers are a case in point. The brothers Eric and John have been successively comptrollers, responsible for the running of the whole of the public side of Chatsworth. A third brother, Joe, was my driver for forty-three years, a most long-suffering man who put up with highly unsociable hours, often working late at night and over the weekends. Their sister married the house electrician. Their father was both my father's driver and mine, while their grandfather was head gardener at Churchdale. All three brothers have children, several of whom have worked on the estate. With the co-operation of the present owners, I recently unveiled a plaque at Eric and John's grandfather's house to mark the vital role the Oliver family has played in Chatsworth fortunes in recent decades.

Another family are the Links. The former head gardener, Jim Link, was the son of a Chatsworth head gardener. In the twentieth century Chatsworth had three successive head gardeners who had each worked in the garden for fifty years (including Jim and his father).

Debo has really been Superpower in building up the infrastructure to cater for the visitors. She is instinctively good on matters of style: someone said to me once that you only had to look at the typography on all the signs to know what league you were in. It was her idea to start the Farmyard, which was opened in 1973. It is intended to explain, in an entertaining but non-sentimental way, the lifecycles and ultimate uses of the commercial farmstock on the estate. It is hugely popular – more than 200,000 people, including 14,000 schoolchildren, visit every season. In 1998 the Adventure Playground was extended and improved and we have special tours and activity days for primary schools. Our latest venture (2004) is to add a new barn to create more space for demonstrations and lectures. And every June 1,600 Derbyshire schoolchildren (nine and ten-year-olds) and their teachers are invited to the park for two free days while each outdoor department puts on a display or exhibition to explain their work. The working sheepdogs, predictably, tend to be the favourites.

Debo was also the instigator of the Farm Shop, set up in 1977 to sell Chatsworth produce direct to the consumer and some other British – but only British – food and wine. There are four shops associated with the house and a percentage of the turnover is passed on to the House Trust in lieu of rent. Then, in the stables, there is the Carriage House Restaurant and Jean-Pierre's Bar (Jean-Pierre was our former chef who was tragically killed in a car accident). The restaurant caters for between twenty and thirty thousand people a month and has three additional rooms for meetings and private or corporate events.

The park – the 6th Duke called it his 'Elysian Fields' – is perfect for large-scale public events. We have the Angling Fair, Country Fair and, latterly, international horse trials, reintroduced very successfully a few years ago by my son and daughter-in-law. All the extra visitors help us to raise significant sums for local and national charities as well as putting some extra in the till for the maintenance of Chatsworth itself.

On the issue of public access to privately owned moorland, I am sympathetic to the aspirations of walkers and ramblers, though I feel on some issues the Ramblers Association have shown themselves a little over-assiduous. Even though their members' reasonable expectations seem broadly to have been met, I suppose owners' reasonable rights are too tempting a challenge. In 1968 I negotiated an agreement for the 15,000 acres of the Bolton Abbey moors with the Yorkshire Dales National Park, which allowed public access with the proviso that the area could be shut to allow shooting for up to thirty days in any one season. We also agreed that the moors could be shut at times of drought to prevent the risk of fire. It was a sensible compromise.

Even so, the possible conflict of interest between those who like to shoot grouse and those who like to walk the moors can easily develop into a class or anti-shooting issue. The precedents went back a long way: in 1932 there was the deplorable incident of the Mass Trespass.

At that time there were no National Parks or legislation to allow access to ramblers. Not a single path crossed the fifteen square miles of the Kinder Scout plateau on the North Derbyshire moors which at that time belonged to my family and was kept strictly private for the shooting. In April 1932 the British Workers' Sports Federation held a weekend camp at Rowarth, near Kinder. They decided to stage a protest against a situation they regarded as completely unreasonable, believing that if they turned out in large enough numbers there was nothing that could be done to prevent them walking the private land. About 400 of them marched from Hayfield to Bowden Bridge quarry, then at a prearranged signal they crossed on to our moorland at Sandy Heys. A line of keepers was waiting for them. Press photographers were on hand to record the confrontation. When the demonstrators made their way back to the road they were met by the police. Six demonstrators were arrested, tried in Derby and, incredible as it seems today, given prison sentences ranging from two to six months.

On the occasion of the seventieth anniversary there was another gathering at Kinder Scout, at which the only protester still living was present. I was invited to attend and took the opportunity to make a public apology for what I could only describe as my grandfather's 'great wrong'. I explained that he had never been his former self after his stroke in 1925 and I didn't think the incident would have happened had he been well. There were fortunately no smart questions like had he closed the prairies when he was Governor-General of Canada, and I could go on to say that I was grateful 'my father was an enlightened man and wanted people to enjoy the park'. And we do too: I couldn't calculate the millions who have come to walk in the park for free since we took over in 1950. We notice, too, that if they find the whole place is tended and loved – and available – they are careful about litter and any form of public nuisance.

In 1951 the first National Park was created in the Peak District and about a year later the first-ever access agreement was signed allowing walkers to roam over 5,780 acres of Kinder Scout and Broadlee Bank Tor. However, some fifteen years ago the issues over access to the East Moor above the house at Chatsworth were different. I had agreed in principle to public access but conservationists raised the objection that this might be a danger to certain species of birds that nest on the moors. It was an issue that I had to ask the Peak Park Planning Board to resolve: now the northern half of the moor has open access, while the southern half has some restrictions.

At the Kinder Scout seventieth anniversary gathering, which was attended by the Rural Affairs Minister, I called on the Government to issue a code so that people knew how to behave in the country: they should be told about proper footwear, for instance, and made aware of the basic rules about closing gates and so on. The Minister, Alun Michael, said he understood the concerns of landowners, and in particular farmers, about the Countryside and Rights of

Way Act of 2000 (which will open four million miles of moor, down, heath and common land for public access in 2005) in relation to signposting and the flexibility to close land if there were genuine concerns for farming, conservation or safety issues.

My views on the right to roam are coloured by my own enjoyment of walking. I went on a memorable walking tour in South America with Robin Fedden and Paddy Leigh Fermor, and again in the Pyrenees and in Greece.

In September 1978 I tackled the Lyke Wake Walk, which takes one across the North Yorkshire moors for thirty-nine miles. We were a party of seven, led by John Oaksey of racing fame and Rupert Lycett Green. The other five of us were not up to their standard and one was unwise enough to be wearing plimsolls – he had to be assisted over the last stretch (not by me, I should add, because I was hard put to it to complete the walk myself). We set out at 5 am while it was still dark and finished sixteen hours later at a hotel in Scarborough. I thought that was a very respectable time: I don't want to hear it's run of the mill for a child carrying two suitcases.

It was exhausting, but as so often with extreme physical endeavour, 'What am I doing?' was soon replaced by 'Thank goodness I did it'. It's the flattery of survival. I have a dark blue jersey embroidered in white with 'Lyke Wake Walk' across its front, which I wear quite often. It is a happy memento of a very long sixteen hours.

I am now eighty-four and very infirm; indeed walking Chatsworth's long corridors is a challenge and on occasion I resort to a zimmer or a wheelchair. I spend the greater part of my time in my sitting room (I was once asked by a journalist why I called it that and not my study, to which I replied 'Because I sit in it more than I study'). It looks westwards across the park with the River Derwent in the foreground. When the weather is right there are picnics on the river banks and children playing games. The sound of their enjoyment is our enjoyment too.

The view from my sitting room is not only beautiful but the essential reminder of my good fortune. Chatsworth, with all its variety of activities, is as lovely a place as you will find. It keeps me conscious that no matter how hard I have tried I can never repay the good fortune that has been bestowed on me. The capricious chance of the sniper's bullet in September 1944 would anyway have imposed obligations on that good fortune. I ask no more of life than to look out of the windows at the beauty of the park, so greatly added to by the fact that countless numbers of people can share its pleasure with me.